THE NEW COMPLETE

BABYSITTER'S HANDBOOK

by Carol Barkin & Elizabeth James
Illustrated by Martha Weston

Clarion Books/New York

This book is intended to provide a comprehensive overview of babysitting.
Neither the publisher nor the authors are engaged in rendering general
medical advice or advice regarding medical emergencies. If medical or
other expert assistance is needed in any particular situation, the services
of a competent professional should be sought.

Clarion Books
a Houghton Mifflin Company imprint
215 Park Avenue South, New York, NY 10003
Text copyright © 1995 by Carol Barkin and Elizabeth James
Illustrations copyright © 1995 by Martha Weston

Portions of this book were previously published in *The Complete Babysitter's
Handbook* (Simon & Schuster), copyright © 1980 by Carol Barkin and
Elizabeth James

The illustrations for this book were executed in pen and ink
and watercolor wash.
The text was set in 11/14-point Baskerville.

Printed in the USA

Library of Congress Cataloging-in-Publication Data

Barkin, Carol.
        The new complete babysitter's handbook / by Carol Barkin and
Elizabeth James ; illustrated by Martha Weston.
                p.   cm.
        Includes index.
        ISBN 0-395-66557-4   PA ISBN 0-395-66558-2
        1. Babysitting–Juvenile literature.   I. James, Elizabeth.   II.
Weston, Martha.   III. Title.
        HQ769.5.B38   1994
        649'.1'0248–dc20   93-39345
                                                              CIP
                                                               AC

            VB   10 9 8 7 6 5 4 3 2 1

TO OUR PARENTS,
who encouraged us to be babysitters,

and

TO OUR BROTHERS AND SISTER,
who suffered through our first attempts

ACKNOWLEDGMENTS

We extend our grateful appreciation to Ms. Pat Purello, Administrative Director of the Hudson Valley Poison Center, for reading the sections of the book that concern accidental poisoning and for giving us suggestions to improve and clarify them. We are also very grateful to Thomas K. Aldrich, M.D., Professor of Medicine, Albert Einstein College of Medicine; Stephen P. Kelly, M.D., A.A.F.P.; and Robert S. Klein, M.D., Professor of Medicine, Epidemiology, and Social Medicine, Albert Einstein College of Medicine, for their critical reading of the sections on first aid and emergencies and their invaluable help in making these sections understandable to our readers.

CONTENTS

Chapter 4

Chapter 5

Chapter 6

Chapter 7

Appendix B

Appendix C

CHAPTER 1

The Most Popular Babysitter in Town

Of all the available babysitters, what will make you the person Mrs. Jones calls first?

Everyone's favorite babysitter is the one who really enjoys the job. And the best part of babysitting is that the more fun you have doing it, the more jobs you'll get.

It may seem surprising that by having more

fun, you'll get more work. But it's true! If you have a good time with the kids you're sitting for, chances are they're happy, too. They'll want to see you again, and they'll let their parents know.

Are you worried that you can't compete for jobs with experienced grandmotherly types? Don't be. Teenagers have many advantages. You have much more energy than an older person, and that's a big plus when you're dealing with young children. Also, you're not very many years older than your charges. You can probably remember what made you happy and sad when you were little; that helps you understand how the kids you are sitting for feel. Finally, don't forget that children tend to hero-worship older kids, which can make your job much easier.

Babysitting isn't just for girls. Traditionally, taking care of children was "women's work" in our society. But luckily, things have changed. These days, many boys enjoy babysitting and they are often in demand. Some little boys prefer male babysitters; they like having a big guy to follow around and look up to.

Of course, anyone who babysits has to take the responsibilities seriously. Parents must feel confident about leaving their children's safety and well-being in your hands.

What else do parents look for in a babysitter?

You can probably think of a number of things yourself: friendliness, interest in younger children, honesty, punctuality, the ability to be kind but firm, respect for other people's privacy and possessions, sensitivity to children's needs, and a good supply of common sense.

Attitude is everything in this job. When parents know that you like taking care of their children and when they know they can trust you to do a professional job, you'll have more work than you can handle.

CHAPTER 2

Is Babysitting the Right Job for You?

Babysitting is a great way to earn money. It's one of the few jobs that is always available. Wherever there are families with young children, babysitters are needed. And it's not full-time work. There are babysitting jobs to fit almost any schedule.

But before you plunge in, think over the pros and cons of this kind of work.

Is It Okay with Your Parents?

While you're in school and living at home, you need your parents' cooperation for any kind of job you want to do. Go over the family ground rules with your parents. Do they object to weeknight babysitting? What about weekends—can you take a job that will last until two in the morning or do you have to be home by midnight?

Your parents may be concerned that babysitting jobs will take too much time away from your homework. Or they may want you to be available to take care of your own younger brothers and sisters. Maybe your family does things together every weekend and they won't be happy about your not being with them.

Whatever their questions, talk things over and make sure you're all in agreement. Getting your parents in your corner is the best start for your babysitting career.

Do You Have Time to Babysit?

Babysitting does take time, and you may not have much to spare. For example, are your afternoons free for babysitting, or are you all tied up with music lessons, swim team practice, drama club rehearsals, or the student council?

Try to be realistic about how much time you will have for work. You can't count on getting your homework done while you're babysitting. Your job as a sitter is to entertain and take care of the children, and they're not likely to enjoy watching you write your social studies paper. After the kids go to bed, of course, you'll have time to study—but what if this is the night little Debbie has a nightmare?

And don't forget that you have your own social life. You won't have much time for your friends if you take on babysitting jobs every afternoon and evening. Making tons of extra money won't be worth it if you're failing all your classes and your friends think you're ignoring them. So go slowly at first until you see how much work you can handle.

Do You Like Kids?

Think about whether you enjoy being with children. After all, that's the job; if little kids get on your nerves most of the time, then babysitting probably isn't for you.

Do you like children of all ages? You may not know yet which age groups appeal to you most, and of course you won't want to limit yourself too much—you probably won't find many jobs if you decide to sit only with five-year-olds. On the other hand, if handling tiny babies makes you nervous, why not pass up those job opportunities until you feel more sure of yourself around infants? And if changing dirty diapers really turns you off, you'd better stick with children over three years old. You'll enjoy babysitting more if you're realistic about what you do and don't like.

You Know More Than You Think You Do!

Especially if you're just starting out, you may be worried that you won't know what to do with young children. But don't sell yourself short; you have a lot more to offer than you realize. For instance, kids love learning new songs, and even if you can't carry a tune, your enthusiasm is what counts—they'll never notice if you're off-key. And when you sit down to crayon with Josh, your friendly interest and the shared experience matter much more to him than how well you can actually draw.

Simply because you're older, you know a lot more than the kids you take care of. Children are curious about everything, and they'll want to learn new things from you. So go ahead and teach them. It's pretty boring to sit in a chair and watch kids play—you'll all have a lot more fun if you get down on the floor and help them figure out how to build a block tower. Don't be embarrassed to join in and give them the benefit of your experience.

Unexpected Bonuses

Besides being fun and profitable, babysitting can pay off in ways you may not have thought of. First, the experience of looking for jobs and meeting prospective employers will come in handy when you're looking for a part-time or full-time job later on. And of course, babysitting is terrific preparation for other kinds of work with children: summer camp counselor, Sunday school assistant teacher, or summer park–program employee. In addition, a parent you've babysat for often will be happy to write a letter of reference; this recommendation may be very helpful when you're applying for other jobs.

And have you thought about how much you'll be learning while you babysit? As well as finding out about how children grow and develop, you'll be absorbing information about lifestyles that may be different from your family's. You'll probably never again have the chance to be part of the intimate day-to-day life in so many different homes. Keep your eyes open, both for the ideas you'd like to make use of in your own life and for the problems you'd like to avoid.

Once you've decided that you want to give babysitting a try, you're ready to break into the job market.

CHAPTER 3

How to Find Jobs

Are you wondering how babysitters find work? Especially if you're just starting out as a babysitter, you probably don't know how to go about getting customers. But parents of young children are always on the lookout for great people to take care of their kids. And there are lots of ways to let them know you're there and available.

Take a Class

Whether you have experience as a babysitter

or not, think about taking a babysitting class. Usually such classes meet six or eight times; safety and first-aid information may be included, as well as advice about working with children of different ages. You'll learn a lot and you'll feel more confident of your ability to do the job well. Babysitting classes are usually free or very inexpensive, and it's nice to be able to tell a nervous parent that you've completed the course.

The American Red Cross offers its babysitting course all over the country; call your local Red Cross to find out when and where to take the classes. Or try asking at your school guidance office, a community center, or the local Y to find out if a class is offered in your neighborhood. An extra benefit is that whoever gives the class often keeps a list of the people who have taken it; he or she can pass your name on to potential customers. The American Red Cross gives a certificate to everyone who completes the babysitting course. Telling parents that you have the certificate lets them know you take the job seriously. It might even mean you'll get paid a little more!

11

Be a Volunteer

Do you want some practice before you begin your babysitting career? A great way to prepare for the job is to volunteer your time and talent. Go to your own church or temple or to one in your neighborhood; find out if they need someone to watch youngsters while parents attend services. As a volunteer, of course, you'll be working for free. But you'll be gaining valuable experience and making lots of contacts for future jobs.

Other people you might ask about volunteering are your local librarian and leaders of neighborhood Brownie, Camp Fire girls, and Cub Scout troops. Perhaps the children's librarian would like you to read stories to little kids once a week. Again, this gives you a chance to meet prospective customers, and you'll also learn a lot about entertaining small children. Any troop leader or den mother would love to have some help; also, as an assistant leader, you'll widen your pool of families to babysit for.

Don't forget that, as an extra benefit, any kind of community volunteer work looks great on applications for scholarships, student exchange programs, and college admission.

Spread the Word

Word of mouth is probably the best and easiest way to get babysitting jobs. There's nothing better for business than satisfied customers talking about what a good babysitter you are.

Start close to home. If you have neighbors with young children, tell them that you're interested in being a babysitter. After you've worked for a family once or twice, you can ask them to let their friends know that you're available. Other parents are likely to call you if they've heard what a great job you do.

Be sure to tell your own friends that you're looking for babysitting work. Then, if one of them can't accept a job, he or she might recommend you instead. This is an easy way of expanding your contacts with potential employers.

Keep on the lookout for other possibilities. Maybe your family's pediatrician would be willing to recommend you as a babysitter for his other patients.

Get on the List

Churches, temples, Y's, and community service organizations sometimes keep lists of babysitters for their members. Call to find out about this; to get your name on the list, you'll probably have to go for an interview.

One of the best ways to find babysitting jobs is through an employment service for teenagers.

Many communities have such services, run by the chamber of commerce, the town council, or the school system. Usually this is a free listing; you register for the kind of work you want, and the employment service puts you in touch directly with people who have a job to fill.

Of course, you can register for other jobs in addition to babysitting: party aide, house and lawn work, snow shoveling, and even Christmas card addressing! This kind of program is a valuable resource for any community, both for teenagers who want jobs and for adults who don't know who to call when they need help.

If your community doesn't have such a service, encourage someone to set one up. Talk with your school principal, head of your PTA, or someone at the chamber of commerce. You might even find that a group such as Rotary, Lions Club, or Kiwanis would be interested in sponsoring a youth employment program.

Free Introductory Offers

Many magazine publishers offer a few free issues to encourage people to buy a subscription. Why not do the same thing? A little investment of your time and energy can result in lots of new jobs.

For instance, does your community have a

Welcome Wagon or other introductory program for newcomers? Local businesses donate small gifts or discount coupons so that people who are new in town will shop in their stores. Why not ask if you can donate an hour or two of free babysitting to families who have just moved in? Parents will be delighted to have you keep the kids out from under their feet while they unpack the good china or hang the curtains. And you needn't be experienced to do this—you'll be in their home, and they'll be right there in case you have questions. If the Welcome Wagon people are willing to include your service, make up some coupons for them to hand out:

FREE

*2 Hours of Babysitting
in Your New Home.
I'll Keep Your Kids Amused
while You Unpack!*
  Suzie Smith   555-7492

It Pays to Advertise

Advertising your availability to babysit is a way of reaching people with whom you have no personal contact. But for that very reason, it's essential to talk it over with your parents first. They may not want you to work for anyone you and they don't know. Or they may not be happy to have your phone number displayed in a public place.

Your parents may feel it's fine for you to advertise in a place they're familiar with, like your church or temple. If so, find out whether you can put up a flyer or card on the bulletin board. And think about other places where parents of young children often go: a library bulletin board might be a good spot, or the office of a neighborhood nursery school (of course, you have to ask if it's okay to post your ad).

You've probably noticed other people's ads in grocery stores and laundromats. But before you try this, and before putting an ad in a newspaper, make sure your parents approve. They may feel it is too risky to publish your name and phone number to all and sundry. It's not the same as posting your name at church. Anyone who answers an ad from church or temple won't be a total stranger; even if you don't know the family, you'll know someone who does. It's sad but true that in any community there are people whose homes you would not want to go to alone. In your eagerness to find customers, don't forget this fact of life.

Be Creative!

Suppose you have some babysitting experience, but you're looking for more customers? Or perhaps you've just moved to a new city and you don't know anyone yet. Contact the local Y and find out if they need babysitters for the children of people who are taking classes there. If they don't already provide this service, maybe they'd like to start.

Exercise clubs and dance studios may also like the idea of hiring someone to entertain kids while their moms stretch and bend. In fact, many such places already offer babysitting for their clients, and they may need another assistant.

The Movable Babysitter

What if you don't have large blocks of time to sit in someone's house in the afternoons or evenings, but you still want to earn a little extra money? You can offer to take children to places they need to go. Working parents often look for a responsible person to walk a first-grader home or to an appointment after school. Or perhaps a couple of kids in your neighborhood go to gymnastics class on Saturdays. You could take them there on the bus and wait to bring them home.

Once you start thinking of all the places kids go on a regular basis, you'll quickly see that busy parents will welcome your movable babysitting service.

Two-Family Babysitting

Do you know two little kids who are best friends and whose parents need after-school babysitting? Or perhaps two families in your apartment building need child care for approximately the same hours.

It might work out well for you to take care of both children in one home or the other. Naturally, both families will pay you, though you'll probably give them a discounted rate. This not only earns you more than you would get for taking care of one child, but it can be a lot of fun, because the kids have each other to play with.

Babysitting Clubs

You've no doubt heard of the popular series of books called *The Baby-Sitters Club*. But did you know that lots of real-life babysitters have adopted the idea and formed their own babysitting clubs? You can, too. The idea is to have one phone number people can call when they want a babysitter. Whichever club member is free or next in line takes the job.

You can make the rules for your club as simple or complicated as you like. After club members agree on the rate all of you will charge, there are other questions. Do you want to meet at a certain time every week and ask customers to call you then? Do you want to have club officers, and maybe dues? Do you want to make flyers or notices to advertise the service you're offering?

A babysitting club has lots of advantages. Of course, it gives you a chance to get together with your friends. But it also allows you to share tips on babysitting and ideas on what to do with kids of different ages. And once your club is known in the community, you'll all have more work than you might find on your own.

A Party Service

Instead of trying to get regular babysitting jobs, you and a friend might want to start a party service. You'll offer to put on children's parties for birthdays or any other occasion. This takes a lot

19

of advance planning. For each party, you'll be in charge of food and games and probably decorations, too. And the two of you will be taking care of the kids and settling squabbles at the same time.

If this idea appeals to you, start small. Perhaps you could put on a birthday party for your own younger brother or sister and see what's involved. Games that you thought would take up half an hour may last only five minutes. And you might not have realized how messy ice cream and cake can be in the hands of ten five-year-olds. But you'll learn as you go along. And most parents of young children will be thrilled to have someone else take over parties for their kids, especially the cleanup part. If you love parties, this is a great job for you.

Once you start thinking about different kinds of babysitting, you'll probably come up with new variations of your own. Talk with your babysitting customers. Maybe you'll have an idea that's just what they've been waiting for.

CHAPTER 4

First Impressions Matter

When someone calls and asks you to babysit, are you prepared? Or do you sound like this?

You: Hello?
Mrs. Ames: Hello, is this Jane Goodwin?
You: Yes.
Mrs. Ames: This is Mrs. Ames. I saw your ad on the library bulletin board. We're new in town,

and I need a babysitter for next Friday evening. Are you free then?

You: Yeah, sure.

Mrs. Ames: Oh, good. My daughter Laura is just a year old. Have you sat with babies this age?

You: Yeah, I think so. Let's see, the Jones kids—no, they're older. Hm—wait a minute, who were those people? Oh, the Petersons—I think Jimmy is a year old.

Mrs. Ames: Fine, maybe I could give them a call. Do you have their number?

You: Uh—no, I guess I don't. Maybe you could look it up.

Mrs. Ames: Oh. Well, how much do you charge?

You: Gee, I don't know—mostly people pay me what they think is about right.

Mrs. Ames: (sounding doubtful): Okay. We're going to go out at seven o'clock, so I'd like you to come at quarter of. Can you get here yourself? We live at 731 Maple Street.

You: I guess so. I'll probably be able to find someone to give me a ride.

Mrs. Ames: All right. So we'll see you here at six forty-five next Friday.

You: Oh, my gosh, I just remembered—I'm going to my grandmother's for dinner that night. Sorry.

Mrs. Ames is not likely to call you again. And she won't recommend you to anyone she talks to. Naturally, the most important part of babysitting is how well you take care of the children. But if the first impression you give is disorganized and irresponsible, not many parents will feel they can leave you alone with their children. So get it together and sound as if you know what you're doing.

How Much Should You Charge?

Find out from other teenage babysitters what the going rate is in your area so you'll be able to say definitely how much you charge per hour. There is usually an hourly rate that most sitters in a community charge. If you ask for more, you'll lose a lot of work, but if you charge less, you're just cheating yourself.

You may find that there are different rates for different working conditions. Maybe nighttime rates are lower than daytime, since the children are asleep and you can read or do homework. Sometimes the rates go up again after midnight, or on special occasions like New Year's Eve. Or the pay may be higher if there are more than two or three children to take care of.

See what experienced sitters in your community say about rates. Then you can decide how much you want to charge.

Lots of teenagers feel awkward or embarrassed when money is being discussed. And it's easy to let yourself be talked into working for a cheaper rate per hour. But if you know what other sitters are being paid, you'll feel more comfortable about giving people a definite answer when they ask how much you charge.

What Do They Mean by "References"?

When potential customers ask you for "references," they want the names and phone numbers of families you have babysat for in the past. It's natural that people you've never worked for will want to know if you do a good job. So you should keep a list of the families you enjoy working for.

Of course, you can't give out people's names and phone numbers without getting their permission. Next time you work for a family, ask the parents, "May I use you as a reference?" They're likely to say yes.

Also include in your reference list the name and sponsor of any babysitting class you've taken and any other relevant experience (Sunday school teacher, Brownie troop assistant leader, or whatever). Be sure to write down any safety instruction you have had, such as CPR or life-saving classes. Then you won't be fumbling for specifics when you're asked about your qualifications.

Potential new customers may not actually bother to call your references to check on your abilities. The fact that you have this list may be enough for them. But if they do call, a glowing testimonial will get things off to a good start at your new job.

Be Professional

It's essential to keep track of your commitments. The Greens will be really annoyed if you call on Friday afternoon and say you can't make it that evening because of the school band concert—and they'll be even more annoyed if you just don't show up.

Get into the habit of writing everything down on a large calendar. You can sometimes get free ones from banks, savings and loans, or other businesses—if not, buy one and remember to use it. Mrs. Green will have a lot more confidence that you've got your head screwed on straight when you say, "Just a moment—let me get my calendar and check."

Once you've made sure you're free and have accepted the job, write down the family's name and the time they want you in the correct date square of your calendar.

When you're talking to a prospective employer, you'll want to ask some questions of your own. Now is the time to get all the information you need before you get there; jot it down while you're on the phone. Of course, you need the name, address, and phone number of the people you're going to sit for—you'll be upset if you've forgotten how to spell Mrs. Sczymancski's name and you don't have her phone number to call and say you're in the hospital for three weeks with a broken leg!

Besides finding out what time they want you to arrive, you'll need to know approximately when they expect to be home. If you don't know where they live, get directions to their house. And how will you get home? It's customary for the parents to walk or drive you home or to pay for your taxi. Even if you live just around the corner, you should expect this. The people you sit for want to know that you get home safely.

It's also good to find out the ages of the children you'll be caring for and what you'll be expected to do: feed them, bathe them, put them to bed, etc.

Be professional. Ask specific questions and be sure you give clear answers yourself. This will prevent misunderstandings. Besides, it's good preparation for other kinds of work you may do. And write everything down! People are counting on you to be there when you say you will be and to fulfill your part of the bargain. Your employers need to know that they can rely on you.

Get Organized!

As you get more babysitting jobs, you'll discover that it's really helpful to gather all the information about the families you work for in one place. Then you won't be frantically searching for scraps of paper all over the house. You can use a box of index cards or a small loose-leaf notebook; use one card or page for each family, and keep them in alphabetical order.

This is the place to write down the name, address, and phone number of each family you babysit for, and their children's names and ages. You may want to add important facts about the children or complicated directions to the house on these cards. Here's how one card might look:

Mr. & Mrs. James Thompson
14 Sunset Circle
555-9284
Jimmy   age 8
Annie   age 3   allergic to milk products

What About Cancellations?

Presumably you won't have to cancel your babysitting commitments very often. The whole point of keeping a calendar is to avoid conflicts with other jobs or social events. But occasionally a cancellation can't be helped—you might have to go to a funeral, for example, or you might get the flu. Never babysit when you're sick. It's not fair to pass on those bugs to the children, and besides, you won't be in shape to do a good job.

If you must cancel, let your employers know as early as you possibly can. Scout around to see if you can find someone to take your place. Then you'll be in a position to say, "I'm sorry I can't come myself. If you don't have someone else you want to call, my friend Tim Hunter is free that night and he's an experienced babysitter." This way, you will have done what you can to fulfill your commitment, and these parents will be willing to call you again.

A Word About Housework

When you babysit, a certain amount of general cleanup is part of the job. If you fix a meal for the kids and/or yourself, you should wash whatever dishes you've used. And after the children are in bed, you'll put away the toys, games, and books that are scattered around the house. In other words, most parents expect you to clean up any mess you and the kids have created.

On the other hand, doing the laundry, vacuuming, washing the kitchen floor, and shoveling snow are definitely not part of your job. It's always possible that parents you sit for regularly will now and then rush out to catch the eight o'clock show and leave a sinkful of dirty dinner dishes. You certainly don't have to wash them, but if you want to do it after the kids are asleep, it's a nice extra to give your customers. However, if this kind of thing is routinely expected, you're being taken advantage of. Don't do it, or else charge extra for the time you spend on housework.

Your job, after all, is to take care of the children. You can't do that and do housework at the same time. If you find that this is becoming a frequent problem, it's easiest to handle it on the phone before you take the job. You might ask, "Will you want me to do anything besides taking care of the children?" If the answer is yes, say, "I charge more for housework," and figure your rates accordingly. Another approach is to say, "I don't feel I can do a responsible job of babysitting while I'm cleaning the house, so I'll only be able to do it if there's time after they're asleep." You may never run into this problem, but it's just as well to decide in advance what you want to do about it.

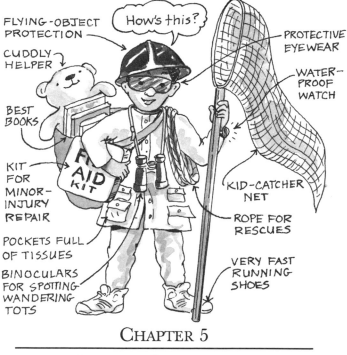

FLYING-OBJECT PROTECTION

How's this?

PROTECTIVE EYEWEAR

CUDDLY HELPER

WATER-PROOF WATCH

BEST BOOKS

KIT FOR MINOR-INJURY REPAIR

F AID KIT

KID-CATCHER NET

ROPE FOR RESCUES

POCKETS FULL OF TISSUES

VERY FAST RUNNING SHOES

BINOCULARS FOR SPOTTING WANDERING TOTS

Chapter 5

Ready for Action

It's five o'clock and your babysitting job starts at six. What do you need to do to get ready for work?

Dress for Success

Babysitting can sometimes be a little messy. Playing on the floor in your dry-clean-only white pants is just asking for problems, and you certainly won't want to feed a drooling baby in your best silk shirt. Wear sensible, washable clothes so you can relax and have fun with the kids. Blue jeans are fine. Parents don't expect you to get all dressed up. On the other hand, they will expect you and your clothes to be clean—and they'll be somewhat put off if you show up in a sexy or otherwise inappropriate outfit.

If you are sitting with babies, don't wear necklaces, pointed pins, or dangly earrings. Little babies can clutch onto these shimmering items faster and more tenaciously than you might think is possible.

Get Ready to Go

Think about what you want to take with you on the job. If the children are going to be asleep, you'll probably have time to do some homework, read a book, or work on that sweater you're knitting for Dad.

A pen or pencil is useful to take with you, in case you can't find one when you need to take a phone message. And it's a good idea to invest in a small flashlight and carry it in your pocket or purse. If there's a power failure or even a burntout light bulb, you won't want to fumble around searching for a flashlight in a strange house. Remember, too, that since you won't be in your own home, you should take an extra sweater with

you if you think it might be drafty. Keep a few
Band-Aids in your wallet or purse—they often
come in handy.

Don't walk out of your house completely pen-
niless. Be sure you have a little money with you.
That way you'll have change if it's necessary
when the parents pay you. This is something a lot
of sitters don't think of doing, and parents notice
this kind of thoughtfulness. Another reason to
have some money with you is in case of emergency. What if the bus breaks down on the way
to your job and you need to call and let them
know you'll be late?

Of course, you'll take along the name, address,
and phone number of the people you're sitting
for. Even if you know them by heart, you might
get flustered in an emergency when you need to
tell someone where you are. If your community
doesn't have 911 service, write down the emergency phone numbers for your fire department,
police department, and Emergency Medical
Service (EMS). Write down the number of the
poison control center, whether you have 911 service or not.

Also include the name and phone number of
your family doctor; this is your own personal
emergency list, and if for some reason you'can't
reach a child's own doctor, it's good to have

someone else to call. And don't forget to put your own home phone number on this paper; it may seem a little silly, but in an emergency your mind may go blank. You'll probably never need to use any of these numbers, but it's reassuring to have them all with you, just in case.

Before you go out the door, be sure to leave a note for your parents with the name, address, and phone number of the people you're sitting for and the time you expect to be home. This is common sense as well as common courtesy.

Allow yourself enough time to arrive promptly, or even a few minutes early. This will give you a chance to say hi to the kids before their parents go out and to get any last-minute instructions. The parents will want to leave at the time they've planned on, so your promptness will be appreciated.

Something Extra—A Surprise Bag

How about putting together a surprise bag as part of your babysitting equipment? Nothing breaks the ice faster with children than something new to play with, and your collection will help distract them as their parents leave.

You can do this for practically nothing. Use your imagination, and rescue potential playthings before they're thrown into the trash. Keep on the lookout for:

- disposable aluminum baking dishes—great for cymbals

- cardboard paper-towel tubes—terrific horns or spyglasses or drumsticks for aluminum pans

- plastic lids from coffee cans, etc.—stack them, roll them, use as "stepping stones"

- small cardboard jewelry or stationery boxes, small metal tins (such as tea tins)—fun to open and close and hide things in or great for collecting stuff

- plastic bottles—wash them well and put in a few dried beans or some rice for a rattle (make sure tops are on tight)

If you think you might be outside with the kids, a bottle of bubble-blowing liquid is an inexpensive treat. With the addition of a rubber ball and some pipe cleaners to make animal figures for older children, you'll be the most welcome babysitter in town.

Checklist

As you leave home, run through this list. Do you have everything you need?

- emergency phone numbers
- homework, book to read, knitting, etc.
- pen or pencil
- small flashlight
- extra sweater
- Band-Aids
- money
- surprise bag
- books to read to the kids

CHAPTER 6

First Get the Facts

When you arrive at your babysitting job, everyone is usually delighted to see you. If you've been there before, the kids will greet you with enthusiasm and drag you in to see their latest projects. And the parents will be happy, too. Now they can go out, knowing their children are in good hands.

Important First Steps

One important reason for arriving a little early is that it gives you time to get some essential information from the parents before they leave: the phone number where they can be reached and the phone numbers of their doctor and a neighbor or relative you can call in an emergency. Many families have these numbers written on a pad or bulletin board beside the phone. If not, be sure to write them down yourself. You'll probably never have to use them, but the one time you do, you won't have time to waste paging through the phone book.

It's a good idea to write down the address and phone number of the house where you are baby-sitting; put these on the bulletin board or near the phone. Then, in an emergency, you'll have this essential information ready for the 911 operator.

Ask the parents if they are expecting any phone calls or visitors. If so, write down any messages they want you to pass along.

Getting Your Bearings

If this is the first time you've babysat in this house, you'll need to know your way around. Find out where the light switches are, and how to work the heating system and any kitchen appliances you'll be using. Make sure you know where the children's rooms and the bathroom are, and where their toys, clothes, and diapers are kept. Also find out where the first-aid supplies are.

If the house has a fire or burglar alarm system, you need to know how it works and what to do if it goes off. Another vital thing to find out is how to unlock the doors and the upstairs windows from the inside. In case of fire or other emergency, you have to know how to get out quickly.

Clarify what you're expected to do and when. What time should you feed the children? Do they need baths? When are their bedtimes? Can they watch TV—if so, which programs?

If there is a child still in diapers, make sure you know how to change him. Find out where the clean diapers are kept, what to do with the dirty ones, and whether you should use any baby powder or ointment.

The best way to learn how to diaper a baby is to watch one of his parents change him. But if you don't get a chance to do this, look carefully at how the diaper has been fitted on the baby before you take it off. Then you'll know how to put on the dry one. Hold the baby's two feet with one hand and slip the diaper underneath his buttocks. Then fasten it at the sides. With cloth diapers, be very careful with the pins. Don't put them down where the baby can reach them. And when you stick them through the diaper material, put your hand between the diaper and the baby's skin. With disposable diapers, just check that the

tapes are securely stuck down. Be sure to wash your hands before and after changing a diaper; this is simply common-sense hygiene.

Ask if the children need any medication. A child who has a cold may be taking cough syrup or decongestant, and you have to know how much to give him, and when.

You may sometimes babysit for children who have chronic medical conditions, such as asthma or diabetes. While these kids don't look or act sick, you need to know what to do in case of an emergency. The parents will no doubt explain what symptoms you should be alert for and any medication you should give.

Make sure you understand what to do when the kids go to bed. Do night-lights or vaporizers have to be turned on? Is there a monitor in the baby's room? If so, find out how it works. Go over the children's special routines with favorite stories and toys, and check on restrictions. Can they have juice before bedtime? Are they allowed to throw balls in the house? Are there limits on how much time they can spend with video games or television?

If the family has pets, find out if they will need any attention from you. Do you have to feed the dog or cats or put them out? Make sure you know the rules. Are the hamsters really allowed to run around loose in Tommy's bedroom? Does the Great Dane really sleep in Jenny's bed? Do ask your employers to introduce you formally to any large dog; you don't want him to think he has to protect the kids from you!

Naturally, you can't find out all about the family's day-to-day life in five minutes. But the more you know, the easier your job will be.

In Case of Disaster

Of course, it's highly unlikely that a major disaster will occur while you're babysitting. Still, you are the person in charge of the children, and if something awful should happen, you should be prepared to deal with it. A babysitting class will give you information on how to behave in a disaster. You can also get booklets about disaster preparedness from the American Red Cross and other organizations. Or look in the front of your telephone book—many of them have sections on what to do in emergencies.

Natural disasters like earthquakes, tornadoes, or hurricanes are hard to prepare for. If you live in a region where these things sometimes happen, you probably know the basics of what to do. But in a house you're not familiar with, it's easy to get confused. Ask whether the family has any emergency plans that you should follow. Make sure you know where all the exits are.

If a fire starts in a house where you are babysitting, don't try to put it out. Get the children and yourself out immediately; then call the fire department from a neighbor's house. In a house with more than one story, find out where the fire ladders are kept.

Don't make yourself crazy thinking about terrible things that could happen. Just remember that the most important thing is safety—for you and for the children you're taking care of.

Phone Safety

Obviously, if the phone rings while you're babysitting, you will answer it. It's not a good idea to let the answering machine take all the calls; this means the children's parents, or your own parents, won't be able to reach you if they need to. Here are some hints on phone safety.

Find out who's calling: It's not always practical to pretend the people you're sitting for are at home but unavailable to talk on the phone. However, before you tell someone what time they'll be home or where they've gone, ask who it is—get a name and phone number. Get as much of a message as you can, and try to find out if your employers should return the call that night. Some people don't seem to like to leave phone messages, but do your best.

Don't give out unnecessary information: If the call is obviously a wrong number, never tell the caller the name of your employers, your own name, or the actual phone number he or she has reached. If the caller asks, "What number is this?", your answer should always be, "What number did you want?" Similarly, if he or she asks who you are, say, "Who did you want to talk to?"

This is not being rude. The person on the other end is the one who placed the call, and he knows who he was trying to reach. You have no obligation to tell him who or where you are.

In addition, if someone calls and says he or she is conducting a survey, immediately say you're not interested and hang up. Don't let yourself get drawn into answering questions of any kind; it takes too much time away from your job.

Hang up on obscene or annoying calls: People who make these calls delight in hearing your anger and fear. So deprive them of this sick pleasure. As soon as you're sure it's a crank call, just hang up gently. There's nothing you can do about tracing these calls right now. You might want to jot down the time it happened, and be sure to tell your employers about it when they return.

Try not to let such a call upset you. It is unnerving, but if you hang up calmly, he's not very likely to call back, and he's certainly not going to show up at the door.

Answering the Door

While we're on the subject of safety, here are some pointers on handling people who knock at the door while you're babysitting.

Don't let anyone come inside: Unless it's someone your employers told you to expect or someone you know personally, never let anyone come into the house. You may sometimes feel you're being overly rude and suspicious. But even if a woman says she lives around the corner and her house is on fire, say, "Tell me your address and I'll be glad to call the fire department for you." If it's the man (even in uniform) to read the electric meter, tell him he'll have to come back another time. Your job is to protect the children you're sitting for, and you can't take chances with that responsibility. Better to be overcautious, even if you feel sure the person is telling the truth.

Don't open the door to everyone: Even though you won't let anyone *into* the house, you may feel like an idiot if you're sitting in plain sight by the picture window and the uniformed mail carrier is outside with his official truck at the curb. Use your judgment about opening the door. Keep the chain on if you have any doubts at all, and again, don't let anyone inside. But you can sign for a special delivery letter or a package—the people you are sitting for will probably be glad you did.

Of course, everyone who rings the doorbell is not a mad strangler. But whoever it is usually wants to talk to the owners of the house. Don't feel bad about ignoring the vacuum-cleaner salesman or religious missionaries with free literature—they'll come back some other time.

Remember, although you're alone in the house with the children, you have other people to rely on. Your own parents can give you good advice about anything that worries or confuses you while you're babysitting, so don't hesitate to call them and ask for help.

What Are Your Privileges?

Most of your employers will tell you to help yourself to snacks and soft drinks from the refrigerator. Go ahead and eat, but don't pig out completely—leave them something for breakfast! And do use some judgment. No one will mind if you finish up the potato chips, but they won't be pleased if you eat up all the remaining expensive chocolates from Switzerland.

If the parents don't mention the TV, ask if you may watch it after the children go to bed. This will remind them to tell you about any quirks or special features it may have. Watch whatever you want, but keep the volume down and don't get so engrossed that you won't hear Billy fall out of bed.

And, by the way, if you're the type who gets petrified watching scary movies, don't let yourself start watching one!

As for the phone, any local calls you really need to make are fine, but keep them short and don't overdo it. You can't pay attention to your job if you're involved in a heavy gossip session. And of course, you won't make any toll or long-distance calls—save those for your own phone bill.

What about having your friends come over while you're babysitting? This can be tricky, and families have different attitudes about it. Some employers may feel you should stick to the job and not be distracted by anyone else. Others may not mind at all if you have a friend over to work on a school project or just to keep you company on Saturday night. Almost every parent draws the line at one friend—more than that makes it a party, and that's not what they're paying you for. And don't even consider inviting your boyfriend or girlfriend over for a romantic evening after the kids are asleep. Your employers want to feel that you're treating this as a time to work, not to socialize.

Since you're working in someone else's home, it's up to you to go along with their ways of doing things. The more you find out in advance, the less you'll have to worry about. You'll be free to enjoy yourself and your job, and they'll feel confident about leaving you in charge of their home and their children.

CHAPTER 7

Getting to Know the Kids

When you meet young children for the first time, it's a good idea to take things slowly. Give them time to size you up; try to let them approach you, rather than reaching out to them too quickly. Kids are often a little wary of strangers, especially people bigger and older than themselves. And of course, they know that your arrival means their parents are going out, so they may not be at all happy to see you.

Don't let it bother you, and don't try so hard to make friends that you smother them with phony affection. One way to break the ice is to get down on the floor and start playing with one of the child's toys. He may come over and take it away from you, but at least you've started to make contact. Or you could say, "Gee, this is neat. Can you show me how it works?" Many children can't resist this invitation to show off their skills.

Another ploy is to ask a child, "Will you show me your room?" If you hold out your hand as you say this, she's quite likely to take it and lead you through the house. Children take pride in showing you their rooms, their beds, and so on; since the parents will want you to see where everything is anyway, take advantage of the opportunity.

As a matter of fact, this technique of asking the child to show you where something is or how it works is useful in any situation. It gives the child a chance to show off his knowledge and be helpful; you're much more likely to get his cooperation if you ask for his help instead of telling him what to do. Also, it lessens the possibility of your ending up in a contest of wills with the child—a contest you will probably lose!

While the parent and child are showing you around, keep your eyes open for things they forget to mention. If the child's window is open, are you supposed to close it when she goes to bed? Also observe how the parent deals with the child. If three-year-old Kyle climbs up on his changing table unassisted and Mom doesn't bat an eye, then you'll know it's okay when he does it later.

No parents can possibly remember to tell you everything about their child's behavior and stage of development. So pick up as many clues as you can before they leave. Even in those few minutes, you'll get an idea of how this family does things. Then you'll be able to fit into their routine and not confuse the child with lots of changed rules and regulations.

If at all possible, try to meet babies before their parents leave, even if they will probably be asleep the whole time you're there. You may have to show up early in order to do this, but the effort on your part is well worth it. The baby may wake up, and if she sees a total stranger, she's likely to be upset and scared. Besides, it'll be easier for you to change a baby who wakes up if you've already visited her room and you know where the diapers and clean clothes are kept.

It's only natural for young children to be upset when their parents leave. Don't be surprised if little Ben bursts into tears as Mom and Dad head for the door. This is particularly true of only children, who may feel as though their entire family is abandoning them. It is no reflection on your ability as a babysitter or on the child's feelings for you.

Often the crying stops moments after the door closes. Try picking up one of the child's books and saying, "Let's sit on the couch and read a story." And if he seems willing to be picked up himself, do a little cuddling—it will make both of you feel better. If you've brought along your "surprise bag," now is the time to open it up. There's nothing like making some satisfying noise to take a child's mind off his troubles; try shaking your plastic-bottle rattle or banging two pie plates together. But if he seems inconsolable and won't let you touch him or distract him, don't make an issue of it. Just calmly and cheerfully sit on the floor and start playing with his toys and puzzles. Eventually, he'll stop crying and join you.

It may help to calm a child if you tell her that Mommy and Daddy will be back and she'll see them when she wakes up in the morning. But don't try so hard to reassure her that you tell lies. For instance, don't say that Mommy and Daddy will be back right away. Even a young child remembers what you say, and when it doesn't happen, it will be hard for her to trust you about anything else.

While you are getting to know the child, he is getting acquainted with you. He may be going through a stage of asking rather peculiar personal questions. Don't let this throw you—just answer the best you can and move on to something else. Toddlers are quite interested in the differences between boys and girls and may ask some very straightforward questions. Don't be embarrassed, but answer as simply and matter-of-factly as possible. Similar questions from older children are usually a way of testing you. They know by now that people are sometimes uncomfortable talking about sex, and they just want to see if they can get you flustered. If your response is a calm, "I don't think that's something we need to discuss," that will be the end of it.

As you get acquainted with your charges, keep in mind that everyone likes to talk about his own interests, and kids are no exception. Your enthusiasm about a child's hamsters, stamp collection, or coloring pad will go a long way toward establishing a rapport that will make your babysitting job fun for both of you.

CHAPTER 8

Fun Within Four Walls

For most babysitters, the best part of the job is playing with the kids. You may be surprised at how much fun it is to help a child build a Lego town or give a doll tea party, especially if you haven't done these things since you were little. Some games and toys never seem to change over the years. On the other hand, the children you're sitting for may have some wonderful things to play with that you've never seen before.

Children are very inventive, often devising

their own games and activities. This is great, but if what they want to play seems too dangerous to you, put a stop to it. Even though children generally do know the rules of the house, they might be a bit imaginative in interpreting them to you. If children tell you that a game you feel is dangerous or particularly obnoxious is perfectly okay and Dad lets them do it all the time, say, "Then maybe we'll do it next time. I'll ask your dad," and suggest an alternative form of play. The parents may not, in fact, object to whatever it is the kids want to do. But check first and don't be afraid to say no.

Older children, and even some toddlers, quite often know exactly what they want to play or read. You won't be called upon to come up with entertainment for these children, although you may have to sharpen up your own playing skills! But other kids may be bored with the things they've been doing and ready to try something new. In Appendix C there are suggestions for finding books and stories to take along and read to the kids; this is fun for both you and the children.

Here are some ideas for entertaining children of different ages.

Playing with Babies

Everything is a toy to a baby, even something

very simple. A ring of jingling keys can keep a baby fascinated for some time. Anything you can dangle over the crib or playpen will be a treat. Just make sure it's not sharp-edged or easily breakable, in case the infant gets his hands on it. Since babies tend to put everything into their mouths, the general rule is that anything you give a baby to play with should be at least as big as his fist. Don't let him have anything that he could swallow or choke on.

Babies love bright colors. Try fluttering some brightly patterned cloth as a simple mobile or tie some securely to the rails of the playpen. They also enjoy music and noise as long as it's not startlingly loud or frightening. If you're a secret shower singer, you can be a hit with baby.

For young babies (up to four or five months old), the secret to success is your active involvement. They can't do much themselves, so anything you do for them to watch and try to participate in—clapping hands, playing a toy horn, singing, making faces—will be greatly appreciated. Older babies who are crawling or starting to crawl will love games of "rolling over," bouncing on your knee (baby held upright between your hands), peekaboo, and rolling a ball back and forth. Give these kids a few pots or pans and a wooden spoon to bang with and you'll make their day.

Do you have a debate or part in the school play to rehearse? You'll never have a more appreciative audience than a baby. She won't even care what you say; she's watching your face as it moves and she enjoys the vocal contact, even though she can't understand the words.

Babies are tougher than you think. And warmer, too. If you're comfortable with just a shirt on, little Bobby will be fine without extra layers. He doesn't need to be all bundled up. Of course, you don't want to put a baby down in a draft, but he won't catch pneumonia if he's barefoot. His clothes should be loose enough for him to move around in easily.

If a baby bumps herself, be sympathetic, but don't make a big thing of it. She's got a fair amount of natural padding and is built to handle a number of knocks. She may cry because she's startled or has scared herself, but your happy expression will reassure her that all is okay and she'll soon be grinning.

Babies are often happy just to sit on your lap

and explore your face and hair with their fingers. However, they have a very short attention span. So when the baby starts fussing with boredom, pick him up and give him a look at himself in a mirror, or hand him a set of plastic measuring cups or spoons to play with.

Sometimes a baby starts to cry and can't be jollied out of it. If she doesn't have a wet diaper and she's not hungry, check to see if she's got a diaper pin jabbing her or if her clothes are binding anywhere. At times, there is nothing wrong; the baby is just fretful. Rhythmic motion seems to be the best solution for this. Rock her in your lap or carry her against your shoulder around the room. You can try some gentle jiggling as you walk her. Soft singing may help. And do find out if the baby is teething. Giving her a teething biscuit or the corner of a washcloth to gum on may make all the difference. Another possible reason for fretful crying is that the child is tired. Try putting her to bed or rock her and sing with the lights turned down—maybe she'll just doze off.

Playing with Toddlers

These children (roughly one to three years) are a joy to be with. They are learning new things all the time, and though they can walk and run, you can easily catch them. By age two, many are talking well, and even if not, they can understand most of what you're saying.

Toddlers will stay amused with one activity for a fairly lengthy period of time. But they still can't entertain themselves, and although they may be quick to point out what book they want to read or drag over the toy they want to play with, you'll need to take part in all this activity. Nursery games are big with this age group: ring-around-a-rosy, patty-cake, London Bridge.

Crayons and pencils hold a special fascination, and you may find that "drawing" takes up lots of time. Of course, children this age don't usually care about real pictures and are happy scribbling in different colors. Most toddlers also love to be read to. The two of you can sit cozily together while the child turns the pages and you read the words or point out the pictures.

Other ideas to keep these youngsters happy are imaginary telephone conversations (don't use the real phone); conversations between puppets or dolls; piling lots of small toys in a bigger truck and pushing it around the room; and rudimentary forms of hide-and-seek. Little kids like to help you; you can make a game of picking up the toys and putting them away.

A toddler's life is full of bumps and falls. If you don't get too concerned about these mishaps, he'll probably go right on with what he was doing before. Of course, make sure he's not cut and bleeding. But most kids this age bang into things or fall down a million times without any real injury. If he cries and the injury isn't serious, a cuddle or a kiss to make it better will probably suffice.

Since toddlers are both active and curious, you may sometimes have your hands full. Seemingly innocent things like staircases, electrical outlets and cords, and the cleaning supplies in the kitchen are potentially dangerous to little children. Even balloons can frighten a toddler when they burst, and little kids can easily choke if they put pieces of broken balloons in their mouths. Keeping alert to where the kids are and what they're up to will do a lot to prevent accidents.

People talk about "the terrible twos"; what they usually mean is that some toddlers go through a phase of saying *No!* to just about anything. It's not really fair to call this behavior terrible. Saying no is a child's way of trying to exert some control over what happens to and around her, and she doesn't have many other ways to do this.

The best way to avoid the problem is not to ask yes-or-no questions. If you say, "Do you want to have your bath?", the child is tempted to say no. Instead, say cheerfully, "It's time for your bath!" She's much more likely to go along with you. Even if she still says no, ignore it and continue with the bath preparations. Often the *no* is simply an automatic response at this age, and she'll be perfectly happy to do what you want.

You've no doubt heard of temper tantrums, and if you sit with toddlers, you may witness one or two. Some children take this dramatic way of expressing frustration or overtiredness. Don't be alarmed. Kids don't hurt themselves while they're throwing a tantrum. Either put the child in his room or leave him where he is screaming and kicking on the floor, go to another part of the room, and ignore him. There is nothing you can do for a child while he's in the middle of this explosion.

When the tantrum seems to be tapering off, go

to him with a friendly offer of a drink of juice or another activity. It won't do any good and may actually reinforce this behavior to try to discuss it with the child or even to refer to it. Just pretend it didn't happen and try to interest him in a project he can handle.

Playing with toddlers is mostly a matter of joining in. Take your cues from the child so that you won't involve her in something that's beyond her ability. It's fun to help a toddler learn new skills through play. And think of how proud she'll be when she shows Mom and Dad how she can put her puzzle pieces in all by herself.

Playing with Older Children

From about age four or five and up, kids generally do quite a lot of playing on their own. They may have a project already under way: a model or Lego construction, a large jigsaw puzzle, a stamp or coin collection, or whatever. All you have to do is admire their progress and lend a hand for the hard parts.

If there are two or more children, they often play happily together without needing much assistance. An only child, however, may want you to join in and take the place of a playmate.

But what if the kids are just hanging around saying, "What can we do now?" Think back to when you were their age and see if you can come up with something that will include the whole group.

How about card games? Even younger children enjoy go fish, old maid, war, and sometimes double solitaire. Older children love hearts, canasta, and gin rummy. If you can't quite remember how to play these games, check at your local library and brush up on the rules. Then, if the kids really enjoy playing cards, you can bring your cribbage board next time and teach them how to play.

Most families have a collection of board games, from checkers and backgammon to Clue or Monopoly. If the children enjoy playing, you can spend a whole evening around the board. (Just don't start a game too late—nothing is more disappointing than having to go to bed when you're about to buy Park Place!)

Of course, you'll want to include everyone, so save the harder games until after the little kids have gone to bed. It's not much fun for a five-year-old to watch you and his older sister play Scrabble.

Do you know any pencil-and-paper games? Hangman is a perennial favorite, as are tic-tac-toe and dots-and-squares. Some of these may be new to your charges and they'll be thrilled to learn them, especially when they beat you!

And there are always guessing games. Everyone can have fun with warmer-colder, and you might try twenty questions and Botticelli. Or maybe the children know a game they'd like to teach you.

If you've brought along your crocheting, and nine-year-old Lisa is fascinated with what you're making, why not teach her to crochet? Boys, too, have fun learning a new craft. Your crochet lesson may turn out to be a huge success. Then you can suggest that next time you come, you'll help them get started on a project—place mats for Grandma or a long muffler for Dad. Look around at what's available in the house. Maybe Brian has a new stencil kit and you can spend some time helping him make cards or stationery.

When everybody's tired of sitting still, try some playacting. Older kids love to create and perform skits, with you as the appreciative audience. When there are children of varying ages, you can get everybody involved in acting out

"The Three Little Pigs" or "Goldilocks and the Three Bears." The older kids can help you coach the younger ones, and you'll all have a lot of laughs.

Active indoor games of this kind are fine for working off some excess energy. It's probably best to limit rougher indoor play, especially right before bedtime; sometimes kids get so wound up that they can't settle down and go to sleep. Also, roughhousing can quickly get out of hand. Objects can get broken and heads banged too hard before you know it. Better to be a little over-cautious than to have to tell parents how the lamp got smashed. Don't get drawn into complicated games of hide-and-seek or sardines. It can be pretty scary to lose track of where the kids are in a house you don't know well.

Even when the children are playing quietly on their own, you can't go off and watch television in another room. You needn't keep your eyes glued to them every second, but be aware of what's going on. Children forget that they must not walk or run with things in their mouths or sharp objects in their hands. Remind them to go slowly and to carry scissors and sharp pencils point down. If you're alert, you'll be able to prevent unwanted contact between a running child and a fragile vase or sharp-cornered table.

Keeping the Peace

Like anyone else, children of all ages disagree and sometimes get into squabbles. Either let them work it out themselves or suggest a fair compromise, but don't get involved in discussion or arbitration. It won't help, and if you take one child's side, the other is bound to feel resentful.

If the argument degenerates into actual fighting or a tug-of-war over a toy, you'll have to step in. Turn a deaf ear to cries of "He hit me first!" Just separate them and announce that they must play separately until they can get along. Help each of them get started on another activity. The firmer you are about this, and the less you listen to explanations, the faster it will all blow over.

What if another child comes over to play while you're babysitting? This usually works out fine and can even make your job easier, because the kids are happy. Keep in mind, though, that you're in charge of the visiting child as well as the others. When you enforce the same rules for everyone, you'll all be able to have fun together.

CHAPTER 9

Wide Open Spaces

When you're babysitting in the daytime, it's fun to take the children outside whenever you can. It makes a nice change for all of you from indoor playing, and it gives the kids a chance to work off some surplus energy.

Check with the parents before you take kids outdoors. Especially in big cities, there may be places they're not allowed to go or boundaries they're not allowed to cross. Or perhaps there's a nearby playground you don't know about. Don't forget to ask where the extra house keys are kept, so you won't lock yourself and the children out.

Here are things to consider when you're going outside with children of different ages.

Taking Babies Outside

Babies love to go outdoors—there's so much more to see! They can go out at any time of year, as long as it's not pouring rain. Just make sure they are dressed appropriately for the weather.

In good weather, spend an hour or so in the backyard with a baby. Take a towel or blanket to put on the grass, or use the infant seat. He'll be delighted to look around at the grass and butterflies and the leaves moving in the breeze. Take a few toys outside with you, or let the baby play with natural "toys"—a large leaf, a bright flower, a dry pine cone (don't let him put any of these in his mouth). He'll be fascinated watching you make a clover chain. And if a big black ant crawls over his hand, don't worry about it—he'll think it's the funniest thing that ever happened.

After an hour, the baby will probably be ready for a change of scene. In hot weather, an even shorter time is best, and you'll need to keep him in the shade and watch carefully for sunburn.

Babies also love to go for walks. Of course,

you're actually the one doing the walking—the baby just enjoys the passing scene. She may even fall asleep in the carriage or stroller, but the fresh air is good for her and the exercise won't hurt you!

You can just walk around the block, and the baby will be happy to recognize any familiar sights. But a nearby park or playground may be more fun; even kids who can't join in yet enjoy watching older children swing and slide and dogs chase after Frisbees.

Take along whatever you might need—it's no fun to walk all the way home with a screaming baby just because you forgot to bring the juice bottle. An extra diaper and a couple of the baby's washable toys can keep a pleasant outing from turning into a fiasco. And, especially if baby is teething, take along whatever she's allowed to snack on. Be sure to walk only until you're half-tired—you've got to push that stroller all the way home!

Keep the safety straps of the stroller fastened securely at all times. A stroller isn't a very stable vehicle and can easily tip far enough for the baby to fall out. Older babies want to be escape artists and will try to climb out when you least expect it.

Take special care crossing streets. Carriages and strollers can be hard to maneuver, and either contraption slows you down considerably. You'll need to pay attention to both the baby and the traffic. The baby will no doubt choose the middle of the street to drop the toy you've just handed her (this is why many mothers tie toys securely to the sides of a carriage or stroller).

A stroller doesn't offer a baby much protection and it keeps him much lower to the ground than you are. Watch out for stray dogs or bushes that could scratch the baby's face, and steer clear of tempting berries that his little hands can reach. And of course, never leave the baby alone outside for even a second.

You may follow the same route every day on your way to school. But when you push the baby along it, you'll notice things you might otherwise miss—a striped cat dashing across the sidewalk makes the baby point with glee, and a pair of angry squirrels produces a delighted laugh. A baby makes a great excuse for a leisurely stroll!

Taking Toddlers Outside

Toddlers take great delight in movement of all kinds—running, climbing, tumbling on the ground. You won't have many leisurely moments with this group. You've got to go at their pace, and it sometimes seems they never walk when they can run!

Backyard play doesn't require a lot of equipment. There's lots to keep toddlers amused, as long as you join in and keep an eye on things. Squat down on the ground and look at the fat worms or pretty leaves with him—just stop him before they go into his mouth. A pail or box is a fine place to put a collection of sticks, stones, seed pods, or leaves.

Any time you can spend outdoors with toddlers is a bonus. Even fifteen minutes on a cold day gives them a chance to do all that running and screaming they can't work off indoors. Primitive games of chase and tag are favorites.

Most toddlers can kick and throw a ball, but they're not very good at catching, so try rolling it to them when it's your turn. And they may spend quite a while racing around on a tricycle or other riding toy—just make sure it doesn't get out of control and head toward the street.

If a toddler is allowed to play in the lawn sprinkler, go ahead and join her. Watch out for moving parts, which can cause a nasty bruise. And if there is a kiddie pool, it can be your best ally on hot summer days. Young children never seem to tire of sloshing in water—it may be hard to get them out.

But do be aware of the danger. Countless small children drown every year in six inches or less of water. It's fatally easy for them to slip and inhale a mouthful of water—then they get too confused and scared to push themselves up out of trouble.

So never turn your back on a toddler in a pool, even for a moment, and stay close at hand all the time. Even when he's not in the pool, if there's any water in it the same danger exists. He can race over and fall in while you're retying your shoelaces. Being aware of this potential deathtrap can prevent a tragic accident.

In fact, though it's hard to imagine, a young child can drown in a bucket of water; if she leans over and falls in head first, she can't get out. Every year at least fifty children drown in buckets, many of which are only a few inches full.

71

Toddlers are entranced by water, so it's important to keep your eyes on them.

A trip to the playground is a big deal to a toddler. There's so much to do that she sometimes can hardly decide where to begin. She may go down the slide once, move on to a few quick swings, and then race off to the sandbox. Your job is to keep up with her—it's easy to lose track of one small body in a crowded playground—and to offer help on equipment she can't handle alone. Going down the slide with you a few times may give her the courage to do it on her own.

Playgrounds are not really as fraught with danger as you might think. Youngsters are fairly cautious about using equipment that's much too difficult for them, and the few inevitable falls rarely do much damage. Do be prepared, though, to snatch up a toddler as he dashes in front of the swings. He doesn't know enough to look, and the child on the swing won't be able to stop.

If there's a sandbox, remember to bring some of your charge's toys with you. It will help resolve the frequent disputes over who uses what shovel if you can offer the child her own toy, or trade one for a while with another toddler.

Children this age are sometimes scared of dogs and other animals. It's not surprising; you'd probably be afraid of a dog you had to look up to. Be ready to keep loose dogs away from a toddler, and don't try to persuade him to pet any dog, even one with an eager owner. Children should be allowed to decide for themselves when they're ready to make animal friends.

Kids sometimes want to rest for a bit, sitting on a bench with you and sampling any snacks you've brought along. But often they don't know when to quit playing, and you might have to make that decision for them. When little Emily starts to stumble as she climbs the slide steps, it's time to go home. And of course, you'll be extra careful to hold her hand if you cross any streets.

You may be pretty exhausted yourself after an afternoon with an exuberant toddler, but you'll both have had a great time!

Taking Older Children Outside

Much of the time, children of seven or older have their own "things to do, places to go, people to see." They don't need you tagging along. But before they bound out of the house, be sure all of you are clear about where they can go and what time they have to be home. Let them know you'll be there in case one of them scrapes a knee or needs a peanut butter and banana sandwich. And remind them to put on their helmets if they're taking their bikes.

Younger children (ages three to seven) also may not want you to actually play with them, especially if there's a group of neighborhood friends. But do keep an eye on them to make sure they don't wander off after a lost ball or get into more mischief than they can handle.

If they don't have plans of their own, there are lots of things you can do with older children outside. Build a snowman (of course, you can't do this in July!). Or play some sidewalk games: hopscotch, jump rope, jacks, or "One, two, three, O'Leary." Or just play catch. Budding athletes are often grateful for a chance to improve their catching and batting skills, and you can keep pitching to them as long as your arm holds out.

Kids are curious about how things work, and sometimes you can show them something they've never seen before. If you can find a dishpan or a bucket, a couple of plastic straws, and a string, you can create a giant bubble machine. Use dishwashing liquid and water in the pan for the bubble-blowing liquid. Thread the string through both straws, leaving extra string in between them, and tie a knot in it—this is the bubble maker. Holding a straw in each hand, dip the bubble maker in the liquid and lift it up. Move the straws gently, and you'll form bubbles of different shapes.

If a group of neighborhood kids has congregated in the backyard and they don't seem to have much to do, go on out and get them started on "Simon says." Dredge up your own old favorites and teach them to play "Mother, may I?" or statue-maker, red rover, or spud. You don't actually have to play yourself, but you may be called upon to referee or clarify the rules.

What if it's a beautiful Saturday and the kids

have been glued to the TV set for two hours? Suggest that you all take your lunch outside and have a picnic—the fresh air will do everyone some good!

The parents may have suggested that you take the kids on an expedition—to the zoo, the library, a museum, or even an amusement park. Make sure you have enough money to pay for bus fares and entrance fees and so on. You probably won't be doing this with more than two kids or with very young children, but even older ones can get lost in unfamiliar places. That can be pretty scary for both of you. So stay together and you can all enjoy it.

If you do go out somewhere with the children, it's a good idea to leave a note for their parents. Tell them where you're going and what time you'll return. If you can't get back on time, call and let them know everything is okay.

Swimming with Kids

In the summer, you may be asked to spend a day with the children at the beach or the local municipal pool. This can really be a pleasure! Before you set out, though, make certain you know each child's swimming capabilities and what each one is allowed to do. Can José go off the high diving board or swim out to the float? Must Maria stay in the shallow water?

Of course, there will be a lifeguard, but that doesn't mean you can stretch out and work on your tan or chat with your friends. You're being paid to watch the children and play with them. Kids can get in trouble in the water awfully fast, and you can't be sure the lifeguard isn't worrying about someone else. Be prepared to jump in and pull a child out of danger. It's helpful to take the Red Cross lifesaving class, which is offered at many schools and Y's. And make sure you know where the kids are at all times.

If the house you're sitting at has a pool, find out what the rules are for using it. No matter what, you must be out there with the kids (even older ones) whenever they're in the pool. And make your own rule that when neighbor kids come over to swim, a responsible person must come along to watch them. You can't adequately keep an eye on the whole gang.

The parents of the children you're babysitting for may say it's okay for the kids to go to a neighbor's pool. Again, you must go with them and be there at all times. If two-year-old Miriam is still taking her nap, the others will just have to wait until she wakes up. This may all sound a little heavy, but there's no replacement for a drowned child.

Most kids love playing in water. As long as you keep your mind on the job, you'll all have a wonderful time.

Safety Checklist

Here are some safety rules for taking children outdoors:

- Make sure babies don't put potentially dangerous things into their mouths—such as stones, berries, sticks, and leaves.

- Keep the safety straps of a stroller fastened whenever the baby is in it.

- Never leave a baby alone in a stroller.

- Don't let babies and young children get too much sun.

- Be especially careful when crossing streets with children.

- Keep a careful watch on children in the playground.

- Never leave or turn away from children in or around a pool or other body of water.

CHAPTER 10

Let's Eat!

Like adults, most kids like to eat. So when you're babysitting, mealtime can be a lot of fun. It's great to watch Kimi learn to drink from a cup and to help Kenji make a peanut butter sandwich all by himself. And you may pick up some new and inventive food combinations from the children you're sitting for.

Of course, you'll follow the parents' instructions on what to feed the children. They will probably have told you if one of the kids is allergic to milk products or some other kind of food. But it's never wise to offer children any food that you don't find in their own kitchen. Those cookies you brought with you may contain nuts or eggs or milk products that an allergic child can't eat. Even healthful foods like strawberries or yogurt can cause a severe reaction in an allergic child.

When you're feeding kids, don't be upset if they don't eat much. Some children don't eat as well when their parents aren't around, or they just may not be very hungry that day. Don't try to make them eat. Be encouraging, but let them stop when they want to.

Allow yourself enough time to get the food ready. You should give the kids some warning so they can finish their game while you're getting lunch set up. Younger children can come and play with something at the kitchen table or on the floor so you can keep an eye on them. With any age group, observe elementary safety precautions: keep pot handles turned away from the front of the stove, and don't leave hot pans and sharp knives within reach.

Before preparing food or serving it to the kids (or anyone else), always wash your hands thoroughly with soap. As nurses and doctors will tell you, washing your hands whenever there's a possibility of transferring germs is the best and easiest way to prevent problems. So make sure the children wash their hands before eating, too.

Feeding Babies

If the baby still takes a bottle, find out all about it—how to sterilize or heat it if necessary, how to mix the formula, etc. If you heat it, be sure to test a couple of drops on the inside of your wrist or forearm before you feed the baby. The milk should feel neither hot nor cold to your skin. (Don't use a microwave oven to heat a glass or colored plastic baby bottle; researchers say it can be dangerous. Also remember that microwaves tend to heat things unevenly, so shake the formula thoroughly.)

You also need to know if the baby can hold the bottle herself, and how she lets you know she's thirsty.

If the baby is very young, you'll have to hold him or put him in the infant seat if that's what the parents prefer. To feed the baby on your lap, settle yourself comfortably first in a chair with arms, so you'll have support for your elbow. Make sure there's a washcloth and a clean towel handy, and put the baby's bib on. Hold the baby so his head is higher than the rest of him and he's resting securely against the crook of your arm. Tilt the bottle enough so he's getting only liquid, not air.

When he pushes the nipple out of his mouth, he's had enough for a while. Support him in a sitting position on your lap or hold him against your shoulder and pat or rub his back gently until he burps. (By the way, some babies don't burp. After five minutes if nothing happens, go ahead and put the bottle back in his mouth.)

Some babies bring up a little food consistently when they burp or after they eat. They are not sick or throwing up—it's just that their digestive systems aren't fully mature yet, and they regurgitate some of the food that goes down. Don't let it bother you; just mop it up and go on with the feeding.

For babies who get more than a bottle at mealtime, prepare the cereal or strained food in advance. Then you won't have to interrupt the feeding. Put only small amounts on the spoon and be ready to scrape most of it off the baby's chin and back into her mouth. She'll no doubt manage to get food on her hands and in her hair as well, so keep the washcloth handy.

An older baby may sit in a high chair; be sure he's strapped in securely and wearing his bib. He may be starting to use a cup and a spoon himself, though most of the meal will still be finger food for him. Put very little liquid in the cup. You can always put in some more, and when it spills (it will), you'll have less to mop up.

If you don't get too unglued about the mess, you can have a lot of fun feeding a baby. It's the high point of his day, and he'll love you for being the one who provides it.

Feeding Toddlers

These youngsters do a lot of the feeding themselves, though they may want you to help. If the toddler uses a high chair, ask the parents if he is allowed to climb in and out of it by himself.

Get his meal together before you strap him in; he knows high-chair time is food time and will probably get quite fussy if he has to sit there all ready while you're still fixing his scrambled egg. He may not be able to talk well yet, so stay alert for his half-verbal signals. If he looks around in bewilderment or frustration as you place his meal on his tray, you may have forgotten *his* spoon.

Sit down facing the high chair and offer your assistance if he's having any trouble. You'll probably want to keep his milk glass off the high-chair tray, except when he's actually drinking–his coordination is improving but it's not perfect yet! And don't make too much of spills when they happen. Just mop them up and go on with lunch.

Toddlers can only concentrate on one thing at a time. So try not to play games during mealtime. Laughing or giggling with a mouth full of food can cause a child to choke. Peekaboo can become more interesting than eating, and games can quickly end up with throwing food and cup on the floor.

Some children this age eat a lot and others eat very little. Start with a small amount of food in the child's dish–you can always dole out more. And when she starts pushing the food around and mashing it in her fingers, accept her decision that the meal is over. Just wipe her face and hands and put her down. Cajoling her to eat more won't get you anywhere, and both of you will get irritated. If she refuses everything but she hasn't eaten since breakfast, a handful of dry Cheerios and raisins will put something in her tummy to tide her over until dinner. But don't give a toddler nuts or popcorn or other small hard things to eat. She can't chew them very well and she's likely to swallow them whole or choke on them.

Toddlers are mostly cheerful and enthusiastic. Sharing their mealtime is great fun.

Feeding Older Children

Older children can pretty much feed themselves, but you'll probably have to prepare the food. You may think that what they choose to eat is quite disgusting—dill pickles and peanut butter?—but as long as their parents said it was okay, shut your eyes and give it to them. Just remember all those strange combinations of foods you used to adore!

Youngsters like to feel responsible. They also like to feel they know more than you do. Ask them to help at mealtime. They'll be able to tell you where things are kept and they'll set the table and show you what to put where. Make the preparations a group project, and you'll all be able to sit down and enjoy a civilized meal and conversation.

Easy Food to Make

Usually when you have to feed the children you're sitting for, their mother or father has provided something to give them. But sometimes parents forget, or are delayed in getting home. And sometimes the kids refuse to eat what you planned to feed them. What do you do then?

Don't panic. There's always something in the refrigerator or cupboard. You'll be able to put together a meal the kids will like without filling them up on chocolate bars and cookies. Just keep any food allergies in mind before you decide what to serve. And be very cautious with sharp knives and hot pans around the children.

Cereal

This may not sound like much of a supper to you, but lots of toddlers and preschoolers would just as soon eat cereal any time of day. Slice a banana into it if there's one handy; check the cupboard for raisins and add a handful to the bowl. Then help the kids add as much milk as they want. This is a very easy meal to prepare, and it's also reasonably nutritious.

Canned Foods

Look in the cupboard to see what's available—soup, spaghetti, baked beans, etc. Then check with the kids to find out what they like. Open the can and follow the directions on the label—it could hardly be easier! If you're using the microwave, be sure you understand how it works, and don't put any metal containers in it. Microwaved food heats from the inside out, so stir the food before you give it to the kids—you don't want them to burn their tongues.

Sandwiches

Lunch meat or cheese: Be sure to ask the kids if they want mustard, ketchup, butter, or mayonnaise on their bread.

Peanut butter and jelly: Is there a child anywhere who doesn't like this combo? You might suggest a new treat like peanut butter with sliced banana or applesauce.

Grilled cheese: All you need is a heavy frying pan, bread, butter, and cheese. Put the sliced cheese on top of one slice of bread. Butter the other slice of bread and set it on the cheese, butter side up. Turn the heat on under the frying pan and put in a pat of butter. Then put in the sandwich, still butter side up. When you turn the sandwich over in a few minutes, you won't need to put more butter in the pan. (Tips: If you use a lid, the cheese will melt faster. Put some mustard on one slice of bread for a zing. Try a slice of tomato inside the sandwich.) Grilled-cheese sandwiches and hot soup make a tasty and filling cold-weather meal.

Here's a variation on grilled cheese that's quick and easy to make. All you need are tortillas and cheese. Put each tortilla on a microwave plate or even a paper towel. Arrange cheese slices on top of the tortillas; add a little salsa if the kids like it. You can cover the cheese with another tortilla or leave these *quesadillas* open face. Put them in the microwave until the cheese melts (thirty seconds to one minute). Cut them in strips or wedges and enjoy!

Scrambled Eggs

Allow two eggs for older children, one for the younger ones. Crack the eggs in a bowl, add a little milk or water, whisk it all with a fork. Place a pat of butter in a skillet and turn on the heat. When the butter is melted, dump in the eggs. Mix them around with the fork or turn them over with a spatula when they look "set" around the edges. Stir or turn the eggs until they are cooked. This is a real quickie—it takes about ten minutes from start to finish. Stick some bread in the toaster before you put the eggs in the skillet so it will be done at the same time. If there's fruit in the house (fresh or canned), it's great for dessert.

French Toast

If you can find bread, butter, an egg, some milk, and a skillet, you're in business. Just beat the egg and some milk together in a pie plate with a fork (as if you were making scrambled eggs). Melt a couple of pats of butter in the skillet and dip a slice of bread in the egg mixture so that both sides are coated. Put this bread in the skillet and fry it on both sides until it's golden brown. One egg with milk is enough "batter" for three to four slices of bread. Plan on one or two slices for each child, and don't forget yourself! If you can't find syrup, try spreading jelly or jam or sprinkling cinnamon and sugar on the hot French toast.

Hot Dogs

Are you getting desperate—the kids are starving but they don't want anything you suggest? Look in the freezer. There may be a package of hot dogs. You don't have to defrost them; just slam the package on the counter to break the hot dogs apart. Take out as many as you need and seal the rest in a plastic bag to go back in the freezer. Put water in a saucepan and add the hot dogs. Set the pan on the stove, turn the heat up high, and in about ten minutes they'll be done.

Can't find the buns? Wrap each hot dog diagonally in a slice of bread. If you can find toothpicks, use them to pin the overlapping corners together on top of the hot dog (don't let little kids play with the toothpicks). Tell the kids these are called "pigs in blankets."

What to Do About Choking

Children do choke on food from time to time. Often this is just "swallowing something the wrong way." You've probably experienced this yourself and you know that coughing makes it better. Let the child cough until he feels he can breathe freely, and then wait a few minutes before giving him any more food or liquid. (However, children do sometimes choke on food they can't cough up; if this happens, use the lifesaving technique described on page 143.)

You can lessen the chance of a child's choking by encouraging kids to conform to ordinary table manners. Chew with your mouth closed; don't talk or laugh with your mouth full; take small bites and chew them thoroughly. You've heard these rules of politeness a thousand times, but did you realize that they are safety measures as well?

CHAPTER 11

Bathtime and Bedtime

Bedtime can sometimes be troublesome for children, and therefore for you. It's perfectly understandable that kids who are having fun don't want to miss out on whatever may be going on. Even infants know that bedtime means the end of the bright lights and entertainment.

Some children, too, may feel a little nervous about being alone in a dark room when their parents aren't home. Others may fear that Mom and

Dad won't return—it's hard for them to believe in an event they don't see with their own eyes.

And of course, some kids may just want to see if you'll let them get away with more than their parents do.

However, there are ways of handling the whole bedtime procedure that can make it easier and pleasanter for everybody.

Putting Babies to Bed

One mother came home at midnight to find her five-month-old son crying and the babysitter close to tears herself. "I've tried everything to get him to go to sleep and nothing seems to work! He's fine until I put him down and tuck him in, and then he starts to cry."

The mother took one look at her howling son in his crib, the blankets snugly tucked in on both sides. "Oh, dear, I forgot to tell you. He always kicks and squirms a lot before he drops off, so he hates feeling held down by the blanket—I just leave it loose."

This story has two morals. The sitter should have found out about the baby's sleeping habits before the mother left. In addition, when he didn't drop off to sleep, she should have tried doing things differently instead of trying the same approach over and over.

A baby's world is fairly limited, and each detail of it is very important to him. If you're sure he's not in pain from a diaper pin or an unburped air bubble in his tummy, try changing some of the elements of his sleep environment. Did you put his teddy bear in bed next to him? If you tucked his blanket in tightly, untuck it—he may need to kick his legs freely. Or did you leave him uncovered? Some babies like to feel cozy. Maybe you just forgot to wind up his musical mobile before you turned out his light and left the room.

Babies are usually ready for sleep at bedtime. If you think about what might be bothering him, you can usually fix the problem and he'll doze off happily.

Before putting him to bed, you'll change his diaper and put on his nightclothes (don't forget to wash your hands after a diaper change). You probably won't be giving a young baby a bath; if you are asked to, be sure you know exactly how it's done. Bathing a baby is a tricky and slippery business. A sponge bath with a wet washcloth will do just as well to get the food off his face, hands, and neck.

Get his bedroom all ready: pull the curtains, turn on the night-light or vaporizer and the baby monitor (if there is one), take the daytime toys out of the crib and put his bed companions in.

Now it's time to turn out the light and spend a few quiet moments together. Rocking him in the rocking chair, singing a lullaby, or rhythmically stroking him as he lies in his crib are all good ways to settle him down and provide a pleasant transition from activity time to sleep time.

Nap time for babies is pretty much the same as bedtime, though it doesn't usually involve as much preparation. You'll change her diaper before putting her down, but many children don't wear pajamas for naps. Babies do go through phases of not wanting to nap, so be sure you know what to do if she doesn't fall asleep right away. Some mothers tell you to let her cry herself to sleep, while others prefer that you pick her up after five or ten minutes of screaming.

Once you've sat for a baby a few times, you'll get to know her routine. But at the beginning, follow the parents' instructions as closely as you can. If you love to play with little babies, it's disappointing to have to put them to bed five minutes after you arrive. But don't let yourself be tempted to keep the baby up. She may be very happy to play with you, but her parents won't thank you when she's cranky the next day.

After she goes to sleep, you can open her door so you'll hear her if she cries. Go in and check on her now and then, unless the parents specifically told you not to—but don't go in so often that she can't get a wink of sleep!

Putting Toddlers to Bed

This is the age of complicated and lengthy bedtime rituals. It doesn't mean much to a toddler when you say, "Fifteen more minutes, then bed," but going through her ritual with her gives her the signal that it's time for sleep. Some toddlers have more elaborate bedtime procedures than others, but nearly all have something that's very important to them: saying goodnight to their stuffed animals, turning out the light themselves before climbing into bed, or reading a special story. Find out from the parents what the child's pattern is, since she's probably unable to explain it to you herself.

Most toddlers love baths, so be sure to leave enough time for them to play in the tub. Of course, you must stay in the bathroom with them at all times, so see whether it's all right for the children to take their baths together. Use your own good judgment about bathtub safety: don't let them fool with the hot-water faucet or stand up in the tub. And keep play from getting too active.

You will have found out from the parents how far along the child is in his toilet training and what you are supposed to do. You may have to remind him to wash his hands after he uses the toilet or potty. Then it's time for pajamas. A balky child won't even notice that the pj's are going on if you do "This little piggy went to market" while you're buttoning.

Bedtime rituals can be charming, and cuddling up together with a favorite story book makes you both feel good. But do stick to the parents' usual limits. The child would like you to read every story on the bookshelf, but when you say, "No, two stories is all for tonight," he's likely to accept it without a fuss. He knows the rules, too.

When it's time, give him an extra hug and kiss and then leave the room. Your attitude of cheerful firmness will let a toddler know this is really bedtime, even if he's whimpering a bit. If he gets up, don't try to bargain or compromise—reasoning with this age group doesn't accomplish anything. Don't even think about trying "just one more story." Take him back to bed and give him a little cuddling if he's feeling forlorn; then say good night. Even if this happens several times, follow the same routine—he'll eventually give up!

Putting Older Children to Bed

Even children who can tell time may suddenly forget how as bedtime approaches. Give them some warning: "Bedtime in twenty minutes, kids" will at least give them a chance to finish up their games or projects. Or you can plan things in advance so their baths are taken care of before their favorite television program starts; then you can let them know that when it's over, it's bedtime. Keep an eye on things so that another game or TV program doesn't get underway at this point, providing an excuse to stay up longer.

Depending on their age, older kids may not want you to stay with them while they bathe. Respect a child's wish for privacy. Some kids won't want you to see them naked. But do stay nearby so you can hear them the whole time they're in the tub.

Procrastination is the name of the game with many children at bedtime. You can hold this down to a minimum by moving them along through their bedtime preparations in a positive, cheerful manner. Promise a story or chapter of a longer book or a little chat after they're in bed. Stay with them for ten or fifteen minutes while they get settled and then say goodnight and leave. You can't, of course, make a child go to sleep. But you can get her into bed. Then, if she says she's not sleepy, tell her that's fine, she can just lie in bed with the lights off and think about her plans for the next day or whatever. Don't let yourself get angry or annoyed. You probably did the same sorts of things yourself. Just be firm and friendly—bedtime is the time to get into bed and turn out the lights.

Some children have nighttime fears—of the dark, or of monsters in the closet or under the bed. Don't make fun of these fears or tell the child it's only his imagination. His feelings are very real to him and need to be dealt with sympathetically. Try going with him to open the closet door and look inside. Get out the flashlight and help him look under the bed. Offer to leave his bedroom door open a bit and the light on in the hall, and reassure him that you'll be right there in the next room.

Bad Dreams And Nightmares

Children do occasionally have nightmares. If you hear a child cry or call out in fear after she's been asleep for a while, go in and find out what's wrong. Sit on the bed and hold her; if she wants to tell you about the dream, listen patiently. If you try to reassure her too soon ("There are no dinosaurs in Boston"), you won't get through to her. The dream dinosaur was real to her and she has to get it out of her system. When she begins to wind down, comfort her—assure her that it was only a dream and that you'll be within call if she needs you. You might sit with her for a few minutes if she's still fearful.

Night Terrors

A few children sometimes experience what are called "night terrors." The child may begin screaming in fright, but when you go to him, he can't tell you what is wrong; he hasn't had a bad dream and he doesn't know why he's so scared. A child with night terrors often doesn't fully wake up for a while, and he may seem disoriented and not recognize you.

Night terrors may be more frightening to you than to the child. But it's reassuring to know that these episodes don't last long. Of course, you need to make sure there's nothing physically hurting the child (there rarely is). After that, your only job is to comfort him calmly and gently. He'll go back to sleep after a while, and he may not remember anything about it the next morning.

CHAPTER 12

Babysitting—
A Big Responsibility

When you work as a babysitter, the people who hire you (the children's parents) rarely get a chance to see how you do your job. They'll know if you're mean to the kids or forget to give them dinner, because their children will tell them. But otherwise, you're on your own, and it's a big responsibility.

Babysitting includes entertaining the children,

caring for their everyday needs, and of course, keeping them safe. But perhaps the most important part of the job is one that is usually left unsaid: you will be a role model for the children you take care of.

After all, the children's parents have left you in charge, so for the kids you're sort of a substitute parent for a while. In addition, younger children usually admire teenagers and look up to them. This makes your job easier, because the kids want to please you. But it also makes it harder in a way; if the children like you, they will want to be like you. You're a big influence in their lives. The way you behave to them and in front of them provides a model they will copy.

Courtesy

Children pick up on the *way* you do things, as well as *what* you actually do. If you're rude to someone on the phone or in the park, a child learns that it's okay to be rude. On the other hand, if you explain to Ashley that loud piano playing bothers the downstairs neighbors and that's why she has to stop at eight o'clock, you're providing an example of consideration for others.

Treating the children you're caring for with the courtesy you would show older people makes a powerful impression. Use *please* and *thank you* when you talk to them, and you'll get a lot more cooperation.

That old phrase about "laughing with someone and not at him" applies to children, too. If the one-year-old who's learning to walk takes a tumble and starts giggling, it's fine to laugh along with her. But if she looks upset and embarrassed, don't make fun of her; instead, pick her up and encourage her to keep trying.

This works both ways. When you treat children with respect, you can expect them to treat you with respect as well. A young child pummeling you with his fists probably doesn't mean to hurt you, but it does hurt, and you can tell him that hitting you is not allowed. A pleasant but firm *no* helps him learn to consider your feelings.

Of course, age makes a difference. A two-year-old can't yet grasp adult concepts such as courtesy and fairness. But even little ones notice the difference between angry shouts and pleasant requests. Encouraging an atmosphere of courtesy and respect for others makes your job a lot easier and gives the children a model for their own behavior.

Don't Be a Bad Influence

Whether or not you do things you know are bad for you and/or illegal—smoke cigarettes, drink alcohol, do drugs—it should be obvious that you may not do these things while you're babysitting. All of these destructive habits set a terrible example for children. Even more important, drinking alcohol or doing drugs impairs your ability to think and to do the job you're getting paid to do. And smoking anything is a fire hazard.

When you babysit, treat the house you're in as if you were a guest. Clean up after yourself and use coasters for cups or glasses so you won't leave rings on the tabletops. Don't use the house's fancy equipment like computers or tape decks unless the parents have told you it's okay.

Babysitters are sometimes tempted to snoop around after the kids have gone to bed. Perhaps you have felt the urge to look through the parents' desk drawers and have let yourself think it won't do any harm. Stop and imagine how you would feel if someone went through your desk or dresser and looked at all your private stuff. Stop and consider this, too: parents who discover that you've been snooping (and they usually do) will never hire you again and will tell all their friends that you can't be trusted.

Be Health Smart

Young children are famous for catching every bug that comes along and passing it around to their friends and families. It's a good idea to do whatever you can to keep from catching something yourself or passing your germs on to the kids.

Ordinary politeness and hygiene will help a lot. Be sure to cover your mouth when you cough or sneeze and to dispose of used tissues promptly. Wash your hands before handling food, after using the bathroom, and before and after giving first aid. Just following these health-smart rules cuts down on the number of infections you both give and receive, and it sets a great example for the children.

Common-sense hygiene also helps prevent more serious illnesses. For example, some bacteria and viruses, such as hepatitis A, may be present in human feces; they are transmitted from people's hands to food. You can see that the way to prevent such diseases is to wash your hands every time you change a baby's diaper, help a toddler use the toilet, or use the toilet yourself. It's easy to do this, and it's important.

It's important, also, to check with your parents to make sure that your own immunizations are up to date. There's no guarantee that every child you sit for has had the standard immunizations, and there's no sense in running unnecessary risks. Getting shots probably isn't your favorite activity, but it would be a lot more unpleasant to suffer through the once-common diseases that can now be prevented.

Unfortunately, though, there are diseases that can't yet be prevented through immunization and also can't be cured. The best known of these is AIDS, caused by the HIV virus. One of the biggest problems with such diseases is that infected people don't necessarily look or act sick. They may not even know that they are infected. So there's no way you can simply avoid people with these diseases, even if that were what you wanted to do. Until vaccines and/or cures are found, the best prevention is to follow health-smart guidelines.

HIV is a blood-borne virus. You've probably learned in health class that it is most commonly transmitted through shared hypodermic needles and unprotected sex. Children can acquire it before they are born if their mothers are infected. (Hepatitis B, another virus that can cause serious disease, is transmitted in the same ways as HIV.

However, it is likely that you have been immunized against hepatitis B.)

The chances that you will babysit for a child who is HIV positive without your knowing about it are extremely small, and the chances that you will come in contact with that child's blood are even smaller. Still, because the HIV virus is almost always fatal, you should practice being health smart all the time.

Do your best not to touch another person's blood with your bare hands. If a child falls and cuts himself, of course you'll wash the wound and bandage it. But use a washcloth to clean away the dirt and to gently apply the soap and water; then put the bandage on without touching the wound with your fingers (you shouldn't touch it anyway after it's been cleaned, to avoid passing along any germs you may have). If you're dealing with a serious cut that's bleeding a lot, keep adding layers of cloth as you use pressure to stop the blood; try to avoid touching the cloths that are soaked through. When you're finished, wash your hands well. It's a good idea, also, to keep bandages on any open cuts you may have.

Don't make yourself too crazy about all this. You can't go through life not touching people. Remember that the risk of acquiring the HIV virus in your normal daily life is almost too small to be measured. If you follow the ordinary rules of hygiene, you don't have much to worry about.

Respect a Family's Values

Each family you babysit for has its own ways of doing things and its own set of beliefs. These may be different from the way things are done in your house. But when you babysit, you have to respect the family's values. Even if you don't agree (you may think it's not good for eight-year-old Daryl to stay up watching television till midnight), go along with the way the parents want things done. It's not your job to change or criticize their ways of raising their children.

This applies to religious practices as well. If Mary is supposed to say bedtime prayers every night, don't let her forget them, even if that's not the way you were raised. Similarly, be careful not to impose your own religious beliefs on other people's children.

What about discipline? This is another issue on which families differ. Luckily, most kids try to be good when the babysitter is there so they won't miss out on the fun. But occasionally you may feel you need to enforce a rule. Go easy with this; a "time out"—a few minutes sitting on a chair away from the other children and the activity—usually solves the problem. Never spank or hit a child in your care.

If you often find yourself screaming in anger and frustration at a particular family's children, try to think about why this is happening and how you might get the kids' cooperation. Either find a better way to handle them or don't babysit for them anymore.

Suppose a problem comes up that you're not sure how to handle. Why not call your own parents? Take advantage of that fund of experience they collected raising you and your brothers and sisters. They'll probably be flattered that you ask their advice and they'll be happy to help you out.

Babysitting for Divorced Parents

It's unlikely that you'll go through your babysitting career without working for at least one divorced parent. When Mom and Dad split up, it's always hard on the children; if you've been through this yourself, you know how they feel.

You can't help learning a lot about families you babysit for—sometimes things you'd rather not know. And especially if the separation is recent, emotional tension may run high. Don't let yourself get drawn into the conflict between the parents. A tirade from one parent about the other one's faults and flaws may leave you feeling shaken and upset. Do your best to change the subject, especially if the children are listening. And remember, there are always two points of view in every situation. Try to keep yourself neutral and don't take sides.

The kids may be upset and unhappy about what's happening to their family. Your supportive and sympathetic attitude will help them a lot. In fact, they may tell you things they're unable to tell their parents. You shouldn't push them to talk about their feelings. But if Jerry spills out his fears and unhappiness one evening, he's using you as a sounding board. You can sympathize, but try not to say anything that criticizes either of his parents. You're not a trained therapist; don't tell him how he should feel or how he should be reacting. The best thing you can do for him is listen.

It's important to respect a child's privacy at times like this. Unless what he tells you is so serious (like child abuse) that you feel the police should be notified, don't pass on what he tells you. When he's ready, he'll tell his parents himself.

One thing to consider when you babysit for a single parent is how you're going to get home. The parent won't be able to leave the kids alone and drive you to your house. Make a plan in advance so you won't be stuck without transportation late at night.

Children's Right to Dignity

People who don't spend much time with babies and little children sometimes tend to treat them as if they were dolls. Perhaps you've found yourself saying, "Isn't she cute?" and making sure the baby's outfit looks just right when you take her out in the carriage.

But babies and children aren't dolls. They are real people with their own thoughts and feelings and personalities. Maybe you've heard an adult say to little Amelia, "Go and give Donny a nice kiss," without ever considering that Amelia may not want to. Would this person tell another adult to kiss someone? Not likely.

Children need to be treated with dignity. The more you respect a child as an individual, the more you'll enjoy spending time with him and listening to his ideas as they develop.

Above all, try to recall how you felt when you were younger, and treat your charges the way you would have liked to be treated. Babysitting is full of unexpected pleasures and rewarding moments. One of the best parts is when you arrive to see those smiling faces and hear the kids shouting happily, "Hey, Mom, the babysitter's here!"

CHAPTER 13

Help for Problems

Most babysitting jobs are relatively problem-free. But occasionally something may come up that's hard to deal with. Here is some advice on what to do in difficult situations.

Should You Babysit for Sick Children?

It depends—on how sick the children are and how contagious they may be. For example, if the

112

children have the flu and you babysit for them, you may catch it yourself; this will keep you out of school, away from your social life, and unavailable to babysit until you're better. Also, a sick child can be difficult to care for. In addition to being cranky and out of sorts, he may need medication, special foods, and extra care such as having his temperature taken. In a case like this, babysitting for a sick child may be more responsibility than you want to take on.

Use common sense in making your decision. If the child has a minor cold and you're the type who rarely catches colds, it's probably fine to babysit for her. On the other hand, if one of the children has strep throat, you may not want to take the chance of catching it.

Of course, this doesn't mean you shouldn't babysit for children who have chronic illnesses such as asthma, diabetes, or epilepsy. You can't catch these diseases, and the children don't look or act different from other kids. Just make sure that you know how to deal with any possible emergencies that might occur; for example, ask the parents to explain what you should do if the child has an asthma attack, an insulin reaction, or a seizure.

If you are sick yourself, don't babysit. It's not fair to expose children to your germs, and besides, you won't be your usual alert and cheerful self when you're feeling under the weather. It's also unprofessional; parents aren't likely to hire you again if their kids come down with the flu they caught from you.

What If You Don't Like the Kids?

Don't feel bad if there are a few children you're not very fond of; you can't love everyone in the world. And often the feeling is mutual. Children let their parents know which sitters are their favorites and which aren't, and you probably won't be asked to sit often at a house where you and the children don't have good rapport.

But what if you actively dislike a child you babysit for? This will probably happen to you at least once in your babysitting career. When it does, turn down future jobs with that family. It's not good for either you or the child to pretend that you're best pals. But don't upset the parents by explaining how you feel about their child; there's no need to say things that will be perceived as unkind or rude. "I'm sorry, but I can't babysit for you that night" is a perfectly polite reply. And you never know; by next year, that four-year-old monster may blossom into a wonderful five-year-old for whom you'd love to babysit.

If you find that you dislike a lot of the kids you

babysit for, you need to think about the reasons. Perhaps babysitting has turned out to be the wrong kind of work for you. Or you may be expecting more from young children than they are capable of doing.

What If the Noncustodial Parent Comes Over?

Whenever you work for a divorced parent, it's important to find out in advance what the rules are. Some divorces are friendly, others aren't; it's impossible to know without asking what a particular family's situation is. The parent you're working for should tell you whether the other parent is allowed to visit the children, whether he or she can take the children away from the house, and any other important information.

What if the noncustodial parent shows up unexpectedly and you're not sure of the rules? Because child custody is a legal issue and because divorce often generates such strong emotions, it's best to be extra cautious. Even if Johnny eagerly says, "Oh, hi, Dad," don't open the door and let Johnny's father in. Instead, ask the parent to wait outside while you call your employer and find out what to do. Almost always there's no problem at all, and you may feel a bit foolish and overly suspicious. Still, your first responsibility is to the children, and next time you'll certainly know what the rules are for this family.

Do the Parents Always Come Home Late?

This can be a difficult problem to solve. First of all, make sure you're not contributing to it by being vague about what time you have to leave. Saying, "Oh, it doesn't matter what time you get home," when you actually have a midnight curfew, will confuse the situation.

But if you and the parents agree on a definite time when your job will be over, and they consistently come home later than that time, something has to be done. After all, you're stuck until they arrive; no matter what, you can't just leave. Try explaining that your own parents want you home by a certain time; adults may pay more attention to another parent's wishes than to yours. Another approach is to say, "I love sitting for you, but I won't be able to do it anymore unless I can be home by midnight." This kind of threat is likely to work if you have a good relationship with these people and you're the kids' favorite sitter.

However, sometimes just talking doesn't send a powerful enough message. One sitter's solution was to ask her father to come over at the time she was supposed to leave. Then she did leave, and her dad was there to greet her employers when they finally showed up. Action like this definitely gets your point across, but be aware that the people may be so embarrassed that they'll never call you again.

What If the Parents Say They Can't Pay You?

Anyone can unexpectedly run short of cash, but it's awkward when parents say they'll "pay you next time" and you don't know when that next time will be. It's easy for you, and for the parents, to forget that they owe you money.

You can ask the parents to pay you with a check; however, do this only if it will be easy for you to cash it. Otherwise, the best approach is to write up a bill—use notebook paper or anything you have handy. Put the date, the family's name, the amount they owe, and your name on the bill; make an extra copy for yourself. This way, everyone has a reminder of how much money is owed, and you won't have to do any nagging.

117

Does an Intoxicated Parent Plan to Drive You Home?

What if the people you're working for are drunk when they get home? A person under the influence of alcohol is in no state to drive you home safely, but he or she may not recognize that fact. This puts you in a difficult position. You should never ride home with a drunk driver. On the other hand, you'd rather not embarrass the person by refusing to go with him, and you certainly don't want to get into an argument when he insists he's perfectly capable of driving safely.

It's best not to discuss it at all. Have a pre-arranged signal with your parents so when you call home and say, "I'm ready to be picked up now," your own parents will know that you need a ride and you *don't* need questions about it right now on the phone. If they can't pick you up themselves, they can ask a neighbor to drive over. Or they can send a taxi to pick you up.

This will probably never happen to you. But if it ever does, don't let a fear of hurting someone's feelings make you take chances with your own life.

Does a Parent Come On to You?

Unfortunately, some parents occasionally forget your business relationship and act as though you are their girlfriend or boyfriend. They may make suggestive remarks or sexy jokes, or they may try to touch you in a way that's supposed to be "just friendly" but isn't.

It's very hard to know how to handle this. Often there's no one thing you can specifically complain about. You may be afraid you'll look like a naive idiot if you do complain, and you may wonder if you're overreacting.

But if you don't like the way the parent behaves toward you, you don't have to go along with it. You are entitled to be treated with respect and consideration. A simple statement like "Mr. Jones, please don't do that—it makes me very uncomfortable" will usually stop the behavior without turning it into a big deal. You don't have to explain any further, and it's better not to get involved in a discussion.

Saying you are uncomfortable with the situation should solve the problem. If he was just being friendly, he may think you're oversensitive, but that's all right. If it continues, don't babysit for that family anymore.

What If You Suspect Child Abuse?

Reports of child abuse have increased dramatically in the last several years. Maybe this means more people are hurting children; more likely, it means people are more aware of the problem.

The idea that adults sometimes hurt defenseless children is a frightening one. People want to protect little kids. As they read more reports in newspapers about child abuse, some people leap to conclusions about their neighbors and make accusations that are not true.

There are different kinds of abuse: emotional or mental abuse is possible, as well as physical or sexual abuse. Professionals who work with children find it hard to decide sometimes whether a child is being abused. It's even more difficult for someone like you, who is not specially trained. For instance, did that bruise on Ryan's face come from being hit by an adult or from falling off the monkey bars at the playground? Asking him how he got hurt may or may not reveal the truth.

Accusations of child abuse have very serious consequences. Children may be removed from the home while the case is investigated. Even if the police eventually decide that no abuse took place, the family's reputation is often damaged beyond repair. Because such accusations can do so much harm, you must be extremely cautious about making them.

However, if you feel really certain that a child

you babysit for is being abused, you can't stand by and do nothing. First, tell your own parents about your suspicions. They'll probably have good advice about what, if anything, you should do next.

Another person to talk to is your family doctor. She may have a different perspective on the signs and symptoms you have observed, and she may also have some ideas of what should be done.

If the child is in school, you can make an appointment to go in one afternoon and talk with her teacher. By explaining your concerns to the teacher, you are alerting school personnel to a possible problem. The teacher may say, "Oh, yes, Becky is so accident-prone; she's always falling down and she's broken her arm and a finger right in my classroom." On the other hand, she may simply thank you for talking with her. Teachers are required by law to report suspected child abuse; if she thinks your suspicions are correct, she can inform the proper authorities.

Finally, if you feel you need to talk with some one else, look for the number of a Child Abuse Hotline in your area. You can call and talk with one of the counselors on duty, who will be able to give you good advice.

Whatever you do, don't gossip about the

problem. Spreading unfounded rumors is cruel and irresponsible. And if your suspicions turn out to be true, the family will need a lot of help. Adding to their troubles by telling everyone you know just makes things worse.

APPENDIX A

APPENDIX A

First Aid for Minor Mishaps

Most of the inevitable everyday accidents that befall children are not very serious. There may be a lot of tears and even some blood, but half an hour later the whole thing is forgotten.

If it needs more than a "kiss to make it better" Band-Aid, cold compress, etc.—be sure you tell the parents about it when they come home. A hard bump against a corner of a table may turn into an ugly black-and-blue spot by morning, and the parents will be alarmed if they don't know how it happened. If you're at all worried, call the parents at the number they left for you; explain what happened and tell them how the child seems now. Then they can decide whether to come home early or not. Don't hesitate to do this; even if they decide it's nothing to be concerned about, they'd rather have you be overcautious about their child's safety and well-being.

Here are some common childhood mishaps you can usually handle yourself. After you've performed whatever first aid is needed, you can decide whether it's necessary to call the child's parents or his doctor.

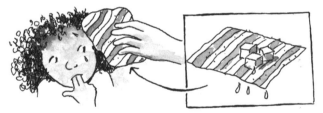

Bumps and Bruises

For the most part, you won't do anything about these. If it's very painful or starting to swell up, hold an ice pack, or some ice wrapped in a dish towel, against the bruise for no more than ten minutes to numb it slightly and decrease the swelling. (Always wrap ice in a clean cloth before placing it against the child's skin.) If possible, hold the ice pack against the bruise for ten minutes every hour; it helps a lot, but some children find the cold too unpleasant to tolerate for long.

Abrasions

Skinned knees and elbows, etc., are painful but not serious. Use a washcloth to clean the area carefully with soap and warm water (be sure to wash your own hands first). If there is dirt, sand, cinders, or the like stuck to the open wound, let the child soak it in the tub or a sink filled with lukewarm water. It's important to get it clean, but you don't have to scrub it hard. When it's clean, pat the edges dry with a towel or clean washcloth. Cover it with a Band-Aid if it will be rubbed by the child's clothes; otherwise leave it open (it will heal faster). Don't put *anything* (iodine, Mercurochrome, antibiotic ointment, etc.) on the abrasion—only soap and water. Be sure to tell the parents about it when they get home.

Cuts

Wash your own hands first. Then use a washcloth to clean the cut with soap and water, and cover with a Band-Aid. If the cut is bleeding more than just a little bit, press a clean cloth to it until the bleeding stops—then wash and bandage.

Some cuts can't be bandaged. For cuts on the lip or inside the mouth, use an ice pack or cold, wet cloths. Scalp cuts bleed a lot, even when they're not very big. You won't be able to bandage them, since the adhesive won't stick to the child's hair. Wash the cut and press a clean cloth over it to stop the bleeding. If the cut is big enough to need bandaging, call the child's parents. They may want to have a doctor look at it and tape it up.

Any cut on a child's face that's more than a scratch should also prompt you to call the parents, since such cuts can leave scars. And a cut around a child's eyes can be potentially serious, so call the parents about those too.

Puncture Wounds

Kids jab themselves with all kinds of things: pins, compass points, any pointed object. Use a cloth to wash the area thoroughly with soap and water and leave the wound uncovered.

If the object was outdoors or if it is large (like a nail), call the parents after you've washed the wound. They will want to make sure the child has had a recent enough tetanus shot. For smaller punctures from indoor objects, you can wait to tell them until they get home.

Nosebleeds

These can happen when a child has a cold or has been sneezing a lot, or he may simply be prone to getting nosebleeds. Have the child sit upright with his head bent forward and his mouth open. Use a clean cloth to gently pinch the nostrils closed and hold them that way for fifteen minutes.

Once the bleeding stops, don't let the child blow his nose or touch it at all. It can very easily start bleeding again, so play a quiet game to keep him from too much activity for a half hour or so.

If the bleeding isn't pretty well stopped after fifteen minutes, call the child's parents.

Splinters

You've probably had plenty of splinters yourself in your life, so you know they are painful but not serious. First wash your hands and the child's skin around the splinter. If the end of the splinter is sticking out of the skin, you'll probably be able to pull it out with tweezers. Don't let the child touch the splinter while you look for the tweezers—he may break off the end and make things more difficult. Clean the tweezers with rubbing alcohol or soap and hot water. Then grasp the end of the splinter and pull it out gently, the same direction it went in.

If the splinter is all the way under the top layer of skin (so you can't grasp the end), just leave it where it is. Wash the area around it with soap and warm water and be sure to tell the parents about it when they get home.

Swallowing Smooth Small Objects

Many children have swallowed small smooth items (such as buttons, marbles, fruit pits, or coins) with no ill effects. As long as the object is not sharp and the child has actually swallowed it (and not choked on it), there's no immediate danger. Take away any other similar items and call the parents to tell them about it. Don't give the child any kind of laxative or other medication.

If the child is wheezing or choking, the object may be stuck in his airway. Call 911 immediately, then call the child's parents. If the child stops breathing, you may have to perform the Heimlich maneuver (see page 144).

Falls

Toddlers and older children fall all the time without any problems. As long as the child picks himself up and is back to his normal playing within a few minutes, there's nothing to worry about.

Occasionally, a child who falls while running full tilt has "the wind knocked out of him." It's scary, because he can't get his breath for a moment, but it's not at all dangerous. Just comfort him and send him back to his game.

Babies also do fall, even if you're very careful. If the baby falls off the bed, don't panic. If she starts crying within a few seconds and has no obvious cuts or broken bones, there's no cause for alarm. Pick her up and comfort her—then call her parents. Even though these falls almost never cause any injuries at all, many parents want to reassure themselves by talking to a doctor right away.

It's possible for a child or baby who falls to sustain a concussion. If the child loses consciousness, vomits, is unable to balance while standing, or is breathing irregularly, call the doctor or 911.

For information on what to do about severe falls, see page 148.

First-Degree Burns

Most children learn the word *hot* very early.

But occasional minor burns do happen, even if you're watching the kids carefully. Such burns only redden the skin and generally do not form blisters. Run cold water on a minor burn for five minutes or so, or hold the burned part in a bowl of cold (not ice) water. This will help stop the pain. Pat it dry with a clean towel and cover it with a nonfluffy bandage. Doctors say you should not apply any creams, ointments, or household substance such as butter to a first-degree burn; don't use any medication unless a doctor tells you to. Let the parents know what happened when they get home.

For information on what to do for more serious burns, see page 149.

Bee Stings

Though painful, bee and wasp stings are not dangerous unless a child is allergic or is stung by many insects at the same time.

For a single sting, it's not necessary to try to pull out or scrape off the stinger from the child's skin; it will fall out by itself if it hasn't already. Simply wash the skin around the sting with soap and water. Then use an ice pack or cold compress to stop the pain. If the stung area starts to itch, slather on a paste made of baking soda and a little water, or try calamine lotion. Be sure to tell the child's parents about it; stings may swell up a lot overnight.

For multiple bee or wasp stings, even if the child seems all right, call the doctor or the Poison Control Center for advice.

Spider Bites

Most spider bites are not dangerous, but three poisonous spiders—black widow, brown recluse, and tarantula—as well as scorpions are harmful to young children. It's a good idea to become familiar with what these creatures look like if they live in your area.

If a child is bitten by a scorpion or poisonous spider, he needs medical attention. Kill the spider if possible so you can take it with you to the doctor's office or hospital. Call the doctor, Poison Control Center, or 911; follow their instructions.

Bites (Animal and Human)

Pets and domestic animals: Nowadays there is little danger of rabies from the bite of the family dog or other household pet. Laboratory-bred pets such as gerbils or hamsters do not carry rabies. But dogs and cats that go outdoors do run the risk of being bitten by a wild animal with rabies. There-fore, if a child is bitten by a neighborhood pet, make certain you know who owns it and where it lives.

Animals carry various kinds of germs, so their bites need medical attention. Wash the bite thoroughly with mild soap under running water for at least five minutes; cover it with a clean bandage. Then call the child's parents or doctor or the Poison Control Center.

Wild animals: There is always a danger of rabies from the bite of any wild animal, large or small. Therefore, don't let children feed the squirrels or play in thick underbrush where they may run into rats, raccoons, or skunks.

If at all possible, the animal should be captured or killed so it can be tested for rabies; if the animal is not rabid, the child will not have to go through the painful series of preventive shots. However, don't get bitten yourself in the process. Get help; call the police and the animal control officers and explain that a child has been bitten by a wild animal.

In any case, if the bite has broken the skin even slightly, use a cloth to wash it thoroughly with mild soap under running water for at least five minutes; notify the parents and the doctor or Poison Control Center at once.

Snakebite: If you live in an area where poisonous snakes are often seen, you should take a class at your local Red Cross or YMCA to learn how to treat snakebite. Do this for your own protection as well as the children's. If a child is bitten, call the doctor or the Poison Control Center or 911 right away and follow the instructions they will give you over the phone.

Bites from nonpoisonous snakes are treated like other animal bites. Any snakebite needs medical attention; try to identify the kind of snake it is. Then call the child's parents or the doctor.

Human bites: This may sound a little strange, but young children do sometimes bite one another when playing in a sandbox or at home. Human beings have many kinds of bacteria in their mouths that can cause infection; first aid manuals say that any human bite that breaks the skin needs medical attention. Use a cloth to wash the bite with mild soap under running water for at least five minutes; cover it with a clean bandage. Then call the child's parents or his doctor.

APPENDIX B

What to Do in an Emergency

While it is unlikely that you will ever face an emergency situation while you're babysitting, it's a good idea to think ahead to what you will do if disaster strikes. You may have learned in school what to do in the following situations. Or perhaps you've taken some special classes, such as a Red Cross water-safety course for a scout badge. Lots of organizations have pamphlets that provide information on how to deal with different kinds of emergencies. See if your local YMCA, Red Cross, scout troop, or Poison Control Center has brochures that would be helpful.

Emergencies are problems that arise unexpectedly and demand prompt action. However, emergencies are also problems you aren't expected to handle all by yourself. Your job is to *call for help* and then do whatever you can until help arrives.

Fire

If a fire starts while you are babysitting:

1. Get yourself and the children (and pets if possible) out of the building. Saving lives is the most important thing you must do; don't stop to use the phone or turn off the TV. And don't stop to see if you can put the fire out yourself—just get everyone out. If you can smell smoke, keep yourself and the children down close to the floor; crawl on your hands and knees to the exit.

2. Call the fire department from outside the house—a neighbor's house, a corner store, a phone booth.

3. Keep the children with you at all times. They are your responsibility until their parents arrive. Stay as calm as you can. The kids will be scared and upset, and you are their only source of reassurance that things will be okay.

Natural Disasters

Earthquakes, tornadoes, hurricanes, flash floods, and forest fires all qualify as natural disasters. If you live in an area where these things happen, you probably know what to do. If you're not sure, though, look in the front of your telephone book; it will give you information about how to keep safe in emergencies like these.

Poison

Lots of household products (bleach, detergent, nail polish remover, medicines, many plants, rubbing alcohol, cosmetics, furniture polish, etc.) are poisonous to children. If a child you're sitting for swallows something that may be poisonous, call the Poison Control Center immediately. The number is listed in the front of your phone book; if you can't find it, call the operator and ask to be connected to the Poison Control Center right away.

Be ready to tell the Poison Control people what the child swallowed (take the container with you to the phone), how old the child is, how long ago he swallowed the poison, and whether or not he vomited after he swallowed it.

While swallowing a dangerous substance is the most common kind of accidental poisoning, children can be poisoned in other ways. If a child you're sitting for breathes in fumes (from an aerosol container or a gas stove, for example) or gets something dangerous on his skin or in his eye, pull him away from the fumes or rinse the skin or eye with clear water. Then call the Poison Control Center for advice and help.

The people who answer the phones at a Poison Control Center are experts on poisons and what to do about them. That's why it's important to call them instead of a hospital or a doctor, who may not have as much experience with all kinds of poisons. It's also important to call them right away before doing anything yourself. The information about antidotes on the label of the poison container may not be completely up-to-date; wait and find out what the experts say you should do.

Follow the instructions you get on the phone. Unless you're told to do so, don't try to make the child vomit, and don't give him anything to drink or eat. Above all, try not to panic. As long as you can tell the Poison Control people what the child has swallowed, the problem can be taken care of.

Medical Emergencies

The best way to prepare for medical emergencies is to take a few inexpensive or free classes in first aid, CPR (cardiopulmonary resuscitation), and lifesaving. These classes are available through the Red Cross at local YMCAs, schools, or community centers. A babysitting class given by your school or fire department may also include lifesaving skills.

You can read about lifesaving techniques in first-aid manuals; you can also find a lot of first-aid information in the front of your telephone directory. But it's almost impossible to learn techniques such as CPR from a book; you need hands-on practice.

Taking a class will help you feel confident that you can handle most emergencies. And parents will be impressed that you take your babysitting job seriously.

Calling the Ambulance

Check your phone book right now to find the telephone number for the Emergency Medical Service in your area; if it's not 911, memorize the number or keep it in your wallet in case you need it quickly. (By the way, make it a habit to say "nine-one-one" and not "nine-eleven," especially around young children. They don't realize there's no "eleven" button on the phone and they have to push the "one" button twice.)

You'll probably recognize an emergency that requires the paramedics if one ever happens while you're babysitting. For example, a child who is badly burned or bleeding severely needs to get to the hospital right away. So does an unconscious child or one who has almost drowned. Even if he has been revived, he must be seen by a doctor. If you aren't sure whether or not you need emergency help, call 911 and let the professionals decide. It's better to make an unnecessary call than not to make one when it's needed.

When you call 911, what do you tell the emergency operator?

- the address and phone number of the house

- the nature of the problem

- the child's age

- that you are the injured child's sitter

- your name and the family's name

Don't hang up; let the emergency operator end the call. If he or she can tell you what to do for the child while you're waiting, listen carefully and follow instructions.

Remember, 911 calls are for emergencies. If you or one of the children has dialed 911 by mistake, don't just hang up without saying anything.

Instead, explain what happened. Otherwise, the emergency operator will have to waste time tracing the call to make sure you're okay.

After you've called 911, call the child's parents and his family doctor. The doctor will either want to meet the paramedics at the hospital or telephone the emergency room to talk with a doctor there.

Calling the Doctor

Even if you don't think a child's life is in danger, you may want to call his family doctor if he has been injured or has gotten sick. You're not likely to reach the doctor right away, especially in the evening and on weekends; you'll get her answering service. Here's what to tell the person who answers:

- first give the phone number of the house you're in

- say that this is an emergency

- that you are the child's babysitter

- that the child is a patient of Dr. X (give the child's first and last names and his age)

- briefly describe what has happened

141

• ask how soon the doctor is likely to call back.

Try to be as clear as you can about all this and don't waste time on unimportant details.

After you've talked with the doctor and followed any instructions she may give you, call the child's parents. Explain what has happened and what you have done so far, and pass on what the doctor has told you. Be as calm as you can so they won't panic needlessly.

Your first concern is always the child, and your attitude can help him a lot. He's probably both frightened and in pain. Your comforting manner will reassure him while you do whatever the doctor advised. If there's nothing to do but wait, sit beside him and keep talking to him. This will make him feel he has help in facing his pain and fear.

Drowning

In rescuing a child who is drowning, time is all-important. Don't waste precious seconds making a phone call; instead, scream for help so neighbors or people in the area will come to your assistance.

If you've taken a lifesaving course, use your skills to rescue the child. If not, and especially if you're not a strong swimmer, be very cautious; you don't want to become a drowning victim yourself, and a panicky child can easily pull you under. For an unconscious child, do whatever is necessary to get him out of the water immediately.

For a child who can listen and then do what you say, extend an object he can grab—a towel, a broomstick, a board, a tennis racquet, anything long enough to reach him—and then pull him in to safety.

Once the child is out of the water, he may need mouth-to-mouth breathing or CPR; these can be performed effectively only by a trained person. As soon as you can safely leave the child, phone for help—call 911, the child's doctor, and his parents.

Choking

If a child has choked on something and can't cough, speak, or breathe, you've got to move fast. There isn't time to call the doctor or anyone else first. Get the child out of her high chair or seat as quickly as possible.

The Heimlich maneuver is performed on a person who is choking. It's best to learn how to perform it in a first-aid class where you can practice before you're ever faced with a real emergency. Lifesaving techniques are very difficult to learn just by reading a book, especially at a time when every second counts. But if you haven't taken a class, read the following description.

MAKE A FIST LIKE THIS. COVER IT WITH YOUR OTHER HAND.

PUSH IN AND UP FOUR TIMES QUICKLY AND HARD.

The Heimlich maneuver involves applying sudden sharp pressure (abdominal thrusts) to the front of the body. For a child over a year old, stand or kneel behind her and put both arms around her. Place your fist against the soft area above the child's navel and below her ribs. Put your other hand over your fist and push in and up four times, quickly and hard. This pressure forces the air out of her chest and along with it the object that is blocking her breathing. You may have to repeat these four thrusts several times.

For an infant less than a year old, sit in a chair; lay the baby face down on your forearm with your hand supporting his face. Rest your arm on your thigh. Tilt the baby slightly so his head is lower than his feet and hit him firmly between the shoulder blades four times with the heel of your hand.

If the baby still can't breathe easily, turn him face up onto your forearm and lower him to your thigh so his head is lower than his chest. Put two fingertips on his breastbone, just below the level of his nipples. Push your fingertips straight in four times.

Repeat both the back slaps and the chest thrusts until the baby is breathing well.

The child or baby may eventually spit out the object or swallow it. In either case, as soon as he is breathing regularly, call the doctor.

It's important to remember that the Heimlich

maneuver should not be performed on anyone who can talk, cry, or breathe, even with difficulty. An unnecessary Heimlich maneuver can do harm.

Electric Shock

Direct contact with electric current can be life-threatening. A child who has suffered a major electric shock may be unconscious or unable to move because his muscles are in spasm.

Remember that electricity is conducted easily through metal and water, and through the body of a person who is still in contact with the source of electric power. Do not touch the child at all until you have separated him from the electric current. Use a dry *wooden* object (pole, stick, broom handle) to push him away from the cord or outlet. If there is water on the ground, put down a rubber mat, a board, a phone book, or a thick stack of newspapers to stand on. Don't use anything made of metal.

It's important to remain calm so that you won't receive an electric shock yourself while you are helping the child. When he is no longer in contact with the power source, make sure he is breathing; use mouth-to-mouth breathing or CPR if you know how to do it. As soon as you can, call 911.

Bleeding

For a child who has been badly cut and is bleeding severely, try to stop the bleeding by applying pressure directly on the wound. Use a sterile gauze pad or clean piece of cloth—dish towel, diaper, sanitary napkin, bath towel—folded into a thick pad to press over the wound. If nothing else is available, use wads of paper towels or paper napkins, or even your shirt. Raise the injured part if possible (for example, rest it on a table) and apply firm pressure. As soon as you can, call 911; keep applying pressure continuously until help arrives. If the first pad fills with blood,

147

add another on top of it—don't remove the first pad, because this may increase the flow of blood. (Don't attempt to use a tourniquet; it is an extremely dangerous procedure when done by an amateur.)

Unconsciousness

The first thing to do for an unconscious child is to make sure he can breathe; if he is not breathing, give him mouth-to-mouth rescue breathing if you have learned how.

For an unconscious child who is breathing, the most important thing to do is keep him still. Don't move him at all except to let him breathe, and don't try to give him anything to drink. Call 911 immediately; then cover the child lightly to keep him warm, and stay with him until help arrives. If he vomits, turn his head to one side and clear his mouth so he won't choke on the vomit.

Severe Falls or Trauma

Serious head or neck injuries can result when a child falls hard or from a great height; other causes of severe trauma include falling off a high-speed bike and being hit by a car. In a case like this, you can't tell if a child has a head or neck injury just by looking at him. The most important thing to remember is to do no harm.

If the child can't get up by himself, don't help him; in fact, don't move him *at all*. Call 911. If it's chilly, take a light blanket to him and cover him; wait with him until help arrives. Paramedics are trained to move injured people who may have head or neck trauma.

If the child gets up by himself, with no help from you, he's probably not badly hurt. Take him inside to rest quietly while you call his parents.

Burns

Anything more than a minor burn requires immediate medical attention. For the most serious (third-degree) burns, in which the skin is actually charred, call 911 before you do anything else. Then make sure the child can breathe; remove clothing from the burn if it will come away easily; cover the burned skin, if possible, with a clean, nonfluffy cloth (a sheet or pillowcase, for instance). *Do not* pull away clothing that is stuck to the burned skin; *do not* put ice or ice water on the burn; *do not* put any kind of ointment, cream, grease, or spray on the burn.

For a second-degree burn (one that blisters) that covers more than a very small spot, place the burned area in cold water (not ice water) or lay a washcloth soaked in cold water on the burned skin. *Then* call the doctor or paramedics. When the pain dies down, gently pat the burn dry with a clean cloth and cover it loosely with a dry, non-fluffy cloth or bandage. *Never* put any kind of grease or ointment or first-aid cream on these burns, and don't try to break the blisters (this can cause infection).

(For first-degree burns, see page 129.)

Other Medical Emergencies

You'll generally be able to tell when a problem is serious enough for you to call a child's doctor or the paramedics. Here are some examples of situations when you should call:

The child has swallowed a sharp or pointed object: Don't give him bread or do anything else. Take him with you to the phone so you can watch for any problems.

The child has injured his eye or ear: This is one time when you don't immediately apply pressure if it's bleeding. It's very hard to tell whether such an injury is serious or not, so keep the child from touching or rubbing it. Take him with you to the phone so you can describe the injury as well as possible.

You suspect the child has a broken bone: Tell the child to stay where he is and not to move at all while you're calling the doctor. Describe the injury as well as you can, and follow the doctor's instructions. Don't try to splint it without instructions.

Remember, in any kind of emergency while you are babysitting, there are people you can call to get help. If you can keep calm and put the children's and your own safety first, you'll be able to cope with just about anything that could happen.

APPENDIX C

Reading to Children

Sharing books with the children you're sitting for is a wonderful experience for all of you. Kids of all ages like to be read to. Although infants usually can't understand the words, they are often soothed by the rhythm of language as you read aloud or recite nursery rhymes. Young children enjoy looking at the pictures and helping you read or make up the story that goes with them. And even children who have learned to read love the experience of a story that's read together.

You can become everyone's all-time favorite babysitter if you bring some books with you to read to the children. A story they've never heard before is an exciting adventure for kids. Of course, you don't have to buy the books. Find some of your own old books, or go to your public library and pick out some that are new to you, too.

For help in choosing books for children, here are some reference books you can browse through. Or ask the children's librarian for suggestions.

Kimmel, Margaret Mary, and Elizabeth Segel. *For Reading Out Loud! A Guide to Sharing Books with Children*. New York: Delacorte, 1988 (266 pages). This excellent book gives information on why, how, and what to read aloud to children. It lists three hundred books for various ages and describes each one so you can tell what it's about. At the back there's a convenient section that cross-references all the books according to age level, topic, length of book, etc.

Lipson, Eden Ross. *The New York Times Parent's Guide to the Best Books for Children*. New York:

Times Books, a division of Random House, 1991 (508 pages).

This huge volume is a list of more than one thousand books for children. They are arranged by age level, with a paragraph of description for each book. Several indexes list the books by author or illustrator, by subject matter, and by type of book. Books the author thinks are especially good for reading aloud have their own separate index.

Trelease, Jim. *The New Read-Aloud Handbook*. New York: Penguin Books, 1989 (352 pages).

This popular book is aimed at parents and teachers. The first half of it is about why it's important to read aloud to children and how to do it; there's a useful list of dos and don'ts. The second part has more than three hundred synopses of books the author feels are great for reading aloud, grouped by age level and type of book.

INDEX